Powered For Purpose

The Barnabas Effect

By Carol Burson

Copyright © 2024 Carol Burson

All Rights Reserved. No part of this publication may be reproduced, distributed, or transmitted in any form or by any means—electronic, mechanical, photocopy, recording, or any other—except for brief quotations of the authors or editor.

Although the authors and editor have made every effort to ensure that the information in this book was correct at press time, the authors and editor do not assume and hereby disclaim any liability to any party for any loss, damage, or disruption caused by errors or omissions, whether such errors or omissions result from negligence, accident, or any other cause.

About the Author

Carol Burson, M.ED, M.S, Servant of Christ

The author of this book has formal learning in the areas of education, counseling, human resource development, and training. Throughout her vocational journey, she has also studied human giftedness and how it can emerge. She would tell you, however, that the credentials she depends on most are not degrees, but God's daily help in working with those He has placed in her path.

This project is about a lengthy conversation with the Lord. It is also a prayer to serve Him by awakening latent treasures He has placed in people. As the writing explores our dynamic inheritance as followers of Christ, it will also share a powerful biblical model for cultivating beautiful gifts, talents, and energies intended for God's purpose. May these words go out to bear fruit. May they serve His pleasure.

Table of Contents

Chapter 1 Where We Are Going 7
Chapter 2 Setting the Stage 10
Chapter 3 The Plot Thickens – The Question of Inheritance 14
Chapter 4 Pointing the Way and Following the Precedent 22
Chapter 5 The Antagonist 26
Chapter 6 Attack, Defense, and Holy Inheritance 39
Chapter 7 The Mission Attacked 47
Chapter 8 Exposing the Enemy 51
Chapter 9 Paralyzed or Powered Up? 58
Chapter 10 The Essence of the Barnabas Effect 65
Chapter 11 The Barnabas Effect in Action 73
Chapter 12 One More Time, With Purpose 78
Chapter 13 Strategic Power of the Barnabas Effect 85
Chapter 14 Leaning into Barnabas Perspectives 91
Chapter 15 Feed These Sheep 96
Chapter 16 Barnabas 101 108
Chapter 17 The Components of Barnabas Business I 118
Chapter 18 The Components of Barnabas Business II 127
Chapter 19 Designing a Barnabas Church That Connects People to Purpose 139
Chapter 20 Conclusion: Seeds Need Help 151
Bibliography 154
Bible Translations Referenced 156
More Resources: 157

POWERED FOR PURPOSE:

THE BARNABAS EFFECT

Chapter 1

Where We Are Going

A wildly famous and popular book began with the words, "It's not about you." And it's not. I invite you to keep that in mind as you open this book, because if you are thinking I am about to give you a step-by-step method to find your purpose in life, please consider exchanging this book for another... perhaps the one that starts "It's not about you."

This book pursues *God's* purpose and the people who carry it. It's about every person who has met God and every person who will meet Him. It's also about how God puts his purpose in His people and the enemy who does not like that plan at all.

To use a sports analogy, this book is about God's people on the playing field of life and how they get hit by the opposition. It is also about countless numbers of God's people who sit on the sidelines. To expand our playing field simile, I will mention a game that many people know. It is simply called freeze tag. I appreciate this amusement because I have used mutations of it in many camps, retreats and training sessions to help people relax and engage and I have found it to be a crowd favorite. I suspect people like it because, in this tag variation, getting tagged does not mean you are out. You are not a big loser for all to gawk at. Instead, you are just deactivated for a moment until one of your team members touches you and frees you to be useful in the game again. There is major comfort in knowing that friends can rescue you and that you can return the favor. I refer to this game because it is a fitting analogy for the subject of this book. My friends, people also get tagged out in the struggles of life. They get frozen and immobilized. In those moments, they often cannot pursue the purpose God has placed in their lives and when that happens, they need friendly rescue. That's why we are about to spend time in this book discovering how to rescue each other and regain our vigor in kingdom work.

I want my readers to take the entire journey through this book, so let's take a moment to get some waypoints. We will soon take an interesting trek through scripture and discover a plot to block God's mission and plunder the resources within His people. Afterward, we will take a turn to explore how Satan has tweaked his strategy for modern life. Then, in the main leg, we will learn from powerful biblical models that can help us counter and return fire with a strategy called the Barnabas Effect.

If we can see the subject of this book within the greater story, we can better understand some challenges that oppose today's church. Knowledge is power, as they say, and what we learn can turn the tide, gain the advantage, and grab the win.

Let's just say it. There is a war going on between our Almighty God and a certain degenerate named Satan, and it involves us. It started in the beginning and it rages on today. That's why it is crucial to stop and pay attention. It's time to regroup, get a game plan, and become a better army of God.

My friends, our efforts won't decide the outcome of this war. The enemy already stands defeated. But make no mistake! We still have high-priority work to do so we can reduce human casualties!

God wants to save precious human lives and activate the treasures He placed in them. Satan wants to immobilize those same lives and render them useless in the campaign. He knows God has gifted each of His children with powerful potential resources for His mission, and that is why he loves his diabolical plan to neutralize human capability in the Almighty's camp.

Today's church is experiencing unprecedented enemy hostility toward its work. The attacks on its mission continue not only from cultural chaos but also from a loss of internal engagement in its ministry. However, the church that can recognize Satan's scheme to steal and neutralize the resources carried within people can also seize a pivotal opportunity to reclaim latent gifts, talents, and energies and restore them to purpose in God's kingdom work.

Fortunately, the church can use God's Word to power up its human resources and take decisive action to drive God's mission forward. Please commit to every step of this journey. It is important, and YOU are needed for a strategic response!

Chapter 2

Setting the Stage

Have you ever watched television coverage of an event where you could see two different scenes and places at the same time? Perhaps you could see a football game going on and, simultaneously, a group of commentators. Or maybe you observed a parade, and you could also see the faces of children along the route.

While the Bible chronicles a history of people in a unique relationship with Almighty God, we can also detect two realms of activity moving along in parallel. There is the dirty, messy, and chaotic progression of mankind, and there is also something going on in the spiritual realm above it. In the beginning, God created. Among other things, He created man, and with a final flourish, he gave him a characteristic called *free will*.

First, let's look at the creation of man on a very elemental level. God made humans because He wanted a family. Scripture says God *is* love, so if man is made in God's image, he must have the innate capacity *to* love. The next element is an obvious corollary. Genuine love is, by nature, *always* voluntary. Love must result from choice. So, if humans reflect God's image, they *must* have *free will* to be capable of real love.

God wants children who love Him with genuine love and who love each other with an *intentional* love that flows from a relationship with Him. We can experience love and distribute it because God placed some of His very nature in us. He wants us to adore Him and to live out our adoration for Him by letting love manifest itself in all our relationships. Love is how we give God the true worship he desires. On the flipside, Satan is everything that opposes and defies God's intentions for humanity. Satan attacks God's people and the plan God has for them. He deploys weapons like perversion, distortion, and carnal confusion and leaves man struggling in a world that is tilted, broken, and warped. Satan attacks what God loves, and what God loves is *us*. We live in a war zone between God and Satan, and the free will of man is the territory at stake.

Yes, there is a war going on! So, in this book, we will explore how to employ the weapons, tools, and maneuvers God gave us for the mission we inherited when we chose sides with our redeemer. Where are these weapons and tools? Well, God's Word holds a formidable arsenal, and when we have God's Word within us, we are strategically armed and positioned to make powerful contributions to the cause.

To begin, let's dig into the origins of war and mission. Satan declared the war we speak of in this writing, and it takes direct aim at man's free will. The fight ensued when God outfitted man with a choice. That little accessory came packed and charged with two words: *must not*.

> *"The LORD God made all kinds of trees grow out of the ground—trees that were pleasing to the eye and good for food. In the middle of the garden were the tree of life and the tree of the knowledge of good and evil."*
>
> *(Genesis 2:9 NIV)*

> *"The LORD God gave the man a command. He said, 'You may eat fruit from any tree in the garden. But you must not eat the fruit from the tree of the knowledge of good and evil. If you do, you will certainly die.'"*
>
> *(Genesis 2:16-17 NIrV)*

Now a certain fallen angel (disguised as a serpent) promptly inserted himself into this story. Mocking God, he said: "That free will thing... Ha! That will never work!" Then he cunningly introduced a despicable little trick.

> *"Now the serpent was more cunning than any animal of the field which the Lord God had made. And he said to the woman, "Has God really said, 'You shall not eat from any tree of the garden'?"*

(Genesis 3:1 NASB)

Right here, we can recognize the slippery slope of questioning God. We can see the error in even thinking God's Word is pliable, negotiable, adjustable, or false. Thus enters a diabolical pitfall called *doubt*.

Here begins the spiritual war against God's good plan for His creation. It targets and manipulates the free will of man, and it will continually wreak havoc on human history. Stay tuned for the Spiritual Super Bowl, pitting God's good and perfect redemption plan against Satan's mockery of it, and then the all-out warfare taking place in the spiritual realm.

After the entry of sin into the story of humankind, God crafted a spiritual objective to draw man to Himself. It had two big guardrails: belief and obedience.

Adam and Eve missed the boat on those two things, and a massive flood showed that scores of other folks did too. In exception, God took Enoch because he walked faithfully with Him, and Noah got a boat to escape mankind's death in the sea of sin. Both men walked in faith. Both men built their lives on a standard of obedience. They *believed God* and obeyed. That was the formula, simple as that.

Next, however, after years of reproduction in the line of Noah's son, Shem, God introduced an incentive to His simple rule of trust and obey. He added a promise and directed it to a guy named Abram, who also believed God and obeyed.

"Abram, get up and go! Leave your country. Leave your relatives and your father's home, and travel to the land I will show you. Don't worry—I will guide you there. I have plans to make a great people from your descendants. And I am going to put a special blessing on you and cause your reputation to grow so that you will become a blessing and example to others. I will also bless those who bless you and further you in your journey, and I'll trip up those who try to trip you along the way. Through your descendants, all of the families of the earth will find their blessing in you."

(Genesis 12:1-3 The Voice)

"*Abram believed the* LORD, *and He credited it to him as righteousness.*"

(Genesis 15:6 NIV)

Bravo, mortal man! You believed!

Forward, man! You were just presented with a promise and a mission that you accepted.

Believe and obey.

There is nothing passive about these words. They are words to be acted upon... then and now.

Chapter 3

The Plot Thickens – The Question of Inheritance

Abram lived in a culture concerned about producing offspring to preserve the family and its assets. He was so behind on this matter that a backup plan was already brewing. Then something extraordinary happened. God showed up and changed the course of history with this conversation:

> *"Do not be afraid, Abram. I am your shield, your very great reward. But Abram said, 'Sovereign LORD, what can you give me since I remain childless and the one who will inherit my estate is Eliezer of Damascus?' And Abram said, 'You have given me no children; so a servant in my household will be my heir.'*
>
> *Then the word of the LORD came to him: 'This man will not be your heir, but a son who is your own flesh and blood will be your heir.' He took him outside and said, 'Look up at the sky and count the stars if indeed you can count them.' Then he said to him, 'So shall your offspring be.'"*
>
> (Genesis 15:1-4 NIV)

This word of the Lord was pivotal. Abram now understood the mission God was presenting to him within the context of his own culture. He would have a male heir to receive a birthright. That changed everything.

For background, Abram's culture operated with a two-part system of inheritance. The two separate parts each served a distinct function in preserving a family line. First, birthright, called the *bechora*, spelled out expectations for 1) leadership and 2) mission. The recipient of the birthright was to embrace the family mission and lead the family members to fulfill it. It was the direction of the father, with specific rights attached. The other part of the inheritance was called *berachot*. These were blessings that included assets like money, land, and property intended to support the family mission. Tradition was to assign these material assets to the firstborn son, who would accept a twofold responsibility. He was to care for all family members and ensure the family enterprise could operate and prosper. (Schlomo Riskin, 16 Jerusalem Post, November 2006). Understanding the role of birthright and blessings is important in the story of Abram because these elements of inheritance establish God as the Supreme Father of the Jewish nation. In Genesis 15:1-4 and Genesis 12:1-3, we can identify these concepts as God forms His chosen family and creates a spiritual sonship in the man called Abram.

Notice that God is saying He wants Abram to become the leader of a nation with a God-given mission. He wants Abram to begin and grow a population that would become God's people. They were to walk with Him in the world, be faithful, and carry out His plan. In time, they would become a great nation. They would prosper and be taught the ways of their Father, God.

> *"When Abram was ninety-nine years old, the LORD appeared to him and said, 'I am God Almighty; walk before me faithfully and be blameless. Then I will make my covenant between me and you and will greatly increase your numbers.' Abram fell facedown, and God said to him, 'As for me, this is my covenant with you: You will be the father of many nations. No longer will you be called Abram; your name will be Abraham, for I have made you a father of many nations.'"* (Genesis 17:1-5 NIV)

God's collective conversations with Abraham guaranteed His people would have specific resources to support this mission. God promised:

- proliferation and protection
- favor and power
- provision of material needs to support this divine mission

As this grand story continues, birthright and blessings will become important anchors for people of faith. That said, let's look one generation forward to a birthright decision that is pivotal in our study.

Now Isaac, who had been privy to all God had told Abraham, became the father of not one son, but two. Before the twins were born, his wife Rebekah knew some kind of war was going on in her womb, and she had the good sense to go straight to God for consultation about this situation. God heard her voice, and He gave her His unvarnished answer.

> *"The LORD said to her, "Two nations are in your womb, and two peoples from within you will be separated; one people will be stronger than the other, and the older will serve the younger."'*
>
> (Genesis 25:23 NIV)

Rebekah took this message seriously, and when the babies were born, she already knew what was implied. Beyond her insight from the Lord, she also saw vast differences between these two boys.

For starters, Esau was born red and hairy. His name meant made or complete, and he was likely a husky, well-developed infant. When he grew up, he was not into farming and flocks, and he deviated from the family business to become a hunter. Further, Esau was a guy who fancied pagan, idol-worshipping women, and based on many conversations reported in scripture, his free will was far from God. *Carnal* is a descriptive word that comes to mind when considering this son who was born first. Moreover, God preferred his brother Jacob even before these twins were born or had done anything right or wrong, and Rebekah was aware.

The book of Romans says it all:

> *"Even before the two sons were born, we see God's plan of choosing. God could choose whom He wanted. It could not be changed because of anything the older son tried to do about it. It was before either one had done anything good or bad."*
>
> *(*Romans 9:11-13 NLV*)*

In contrast to Esau, Jacob *stayed home* vocationally and learned the family business. He learned skills in farming and tending flocks. He was, by choice, a shepherd, and God seems to like shepherds. Based on God's selection of a shepherd boy named David as a King, the Psalm that reads "The Lord is my Shepherd," and the designation of Jesus as the Good Shepherd, there seems to be a distinct affinity for that image in the Bible. Some commentaries call Jacob a *pastoralist* because he managed flocks. Notably, the scripture says of Jacob that he was a *plain man*. The Hebrew word *tam*, translated *plain* in this interesting story, also appears in the book of Job. However, the same word is translated as *upright, righteous, or morally and ethically pure* in that instance. There has been some controversy among scholars about the correct translation of the descriptive word *tam* in the Jacob versus Esau story. To that point, perhaps a different word appears in this story because of the actions taken by Jacob that would seem contrary to *morally and ethically pure*. We must consider, however, that God sees what man cannot. Remember, the Bible says Abraham only had to *believe God*, and God counted *that* as righteousness.

Jacob wanted the birthright. It meant something to him, although he knew little about what it meant. So, one day, when the beasty Esau came home in a hungry rage, Jacob offered to trade him a big bowl of stew for the family birthright. Esau scoffed at the birthright, so he made the bargain and filled his stomach. To emphasize a point, Esau sold his birthright of his own free will. The language of the scripture does not say that Jacob *stole* it.

> *"Now Jacob cooked a stew; and Esau came in from the field, and he was weary. And Esau said to Jacob, 'Please feed me with that same red stew, for I am weary.' Therefore his name was called Edom.*
>
> *But Jacob said, 'Sell me your birthright as of this day.'*
>
> *And Esau said, 'Look, I am about to die; so what is this birthright to me?'*
>
> *Then Jacob said, 'Swear to me as of this day.'*
>
> *So he swore to him, and sold his birthright to Jacob. And Jacob gave Esau bread and stew of lentils; then he ate and drank, arose, and went his way. Thus Esau despised his birthright."*
>
> (Genesis 25:29-34 NKJV)

These words give insight into Esau's spiritual attitude:

> *"Thus Esau despised his birthright."*

Esau was clearly a bigger fan of all things carnal.

Likely, Jacob's mother had, by this time, seen all she needed to see to understand that God's plan was better off in the hands of Jacob than in the hands of Esau, so she wanted Jacob to have the blessings from his father along with the birthright. Did she understand that the *bechora* and the *berachot* should stay together? Is that why she (not Jacob) designed a plan to divert the family blessings away from the beasty boy and over to the son with the birthright? Perhaps Rebekah knew her husband Isaac did not see so well, and in another sense, maybe she knew he could be shortsighted in long-range matters. Rebekah had not forgotten what God had told her about these twins, and she possibly knew what she had to do to follow God's plan. Realizing that Isaac was about to pronounce his blessing, she convinced Jacob to disguise himself as Esau and claim the blessing that belonged to the birthright. Sure, Rebekah might have just preferred Jacob because he did not have foreign wives who were driving her crazy like Esau did. Or could we consider Rebekah could have been *called* to act according to God's plan? After all, everything worked. (An aside: "...together for good, for those who are called according to *His purpose.*") Isaac gave the blessings to Jacob, and the woman succeeded. She kept God's plan on track.

Could we ponder that in the Jacob and Esau story, it is God, not Jacob or his mom, who strips Esau of his *firstborn* position in favor of something about Jacob that He preferred? Scripture explicitly says:

> "For the word of God is living and active, sharper than any two-edged sword, piercing to the division of soul and of spirit, of joints and of marrow, and discerning the thoughts and intentions of the heart."
>
> (Hebrews 4:12 ESV)

It appears Esau is essentially carnal (connected to the desires of the flesh). He scoffs at the spirituality of his birthright because his belly is empty, but he is certainly not opposed to material wealth or power! Note also that he was quite willing to murder his brother when he did not get what he wanted. Esau is not just choosing broth over his birthright. He is choosing a stew of fleshly tendencies, including immediate gratification, pride, greed, jealousy, malice, hatred, and thus a spirit that is not in pursuit of God. Emphatically, God decided not to allow His birthright, which was to play a critical role in His redemption plan, to fall into the hands of Esau. That birthright and all the resources needed for it were directed to Jacob. Certainly, Jacob's flesh was flawed, but God determined that his heart could be malleable for His purposes. Let's also remember that the birthright in question here is not about Isaac's *stuff*. It's about God's *purpose*.

> *"But in order that the choice of one son might be completely the result of God's own purpose, God said to her, 'The older will serve the younger.'"*
>
> *(Romans 9:11 GNT)*

In the chapters to come, we will discuss more about the connection of these early stories to the ongoing struggles of God's people. However, it is prudent here to highlight two extremely important takeaway concepts from the birthright story of Jacob and Esau. These two connections are vitally important today because they relate to Satan's current campaign against God and His church.

Connection 1

First, in this author's opinion, the Jacob and Esau story is not just about two brothers struggling for earthly inheritance. Instead, we can make an excellent case that God is unveiling more of the plan unfolding through the promise made to Abraham. He is revealing a new order to come wherein people will become heirs to the promise, not by birth order or even by birth into a particular tribe or nation. Rather, the condition for becoming a rightful heir to God's promises is a heart pliable to God and the acceptance of His plan (His mission) to bring mankind to Himself. From this point, the scriptures restate and reinforce this idea repeatedly.

Connection 2

The second takeaway is more subtle. In the blessing to Abraham, God guaranteed resources to support His plan and mission. God not only intends to provide material assets as needed, but He will also provide protection, favor, gifts, abilities, strengths, and power to people who enlist themselves for service and leadership. The Jacob and Esau story, then, is possibly a subtle, spiritual hint about an antagonist who opposes God and seeks to disable His plan. He roars about, seeking to steal God's mission resources or separate them from their purpose. We will soon explore defenses against this treacherous enemy who wants to plunder the *potential* God distributes to His people.

Chapter 4

Pointing the Way and Following the Precedent

After many years of struggle, Jacob returned to the place where he met God (Genesis 35). While that is literal in scripture, it is also spiritual for Jacob and us. It is always good to return to where we met God. It is nurturing and healing to hear His voice and let our birthright and His blessings wash us anew. With Jacob, all those things happened, and God revealed a little more detail about a leadership role in a specific mission (*bechora*) and the planned blessings of provision (*berachot*) that He would soon distribute to Jacob and his offspring.

> *"After Jacob returned from Paddan Aram, God appeared to him again and blessed him. God said to him, 'Your name is Jacob, but you will no longer be called Jacob; your name will be Israel.' So he named him Israel.*
>
> *And God said to him, 'I am God Almighty; be fruitful and increase in number. A nation and a community of nations will come from you, and kings will be among your descendants. The land I gave to Abraham and Isaac I also give to you, and I will give this land to your descendants after you.' Then God went up from him at the place where he had talked with him."*
>
> (Genesis 35:9-13 NIV)

In the passing of the years, Jacob would distribute birthright and blessings and apply the principle that inheritance belongs to those with a heart turned to God and His mission. It is not for those who defile it or pose antagonism toward it. He shows an understanding of this principle in the following words to his offspring:

> *"Reuben, you're my firstborn,*
> *my strength, first proof of my manhood,*
> *at the top in honor and at the top in power,*
> *But like a bucket of water spilled,*
> *you'll be at the top no more..."*
>
> (Genesis 49:3-4 The Message)

> *"Judah, your brothers will praise you;*
> *your hand will be on the neck of your enemies;*
> *your father's sons will bow down to you. You are a lion's cub, Judah;*
> *you return from the prey, my son.*
> *Like a lion he crouches and lies down,*
> *like a lioness—who dares to rouse him?*
> *The scepter will not depart from Judah,*
> *nor the ruler's staff from between his feet,*
> *until he to whom it belongs shall come*
> *and the obedience of the nations shall be his.*
>
> (Genesis 49:8-10 NIV)

> "Joseph is a fruitful vine,
> a fruitful vine near a spring,
> whose branches climb over a wall.
> With bitterness archers attacked him;
> they shot at him with hostility. But his bow remained steady,

> his strong arms stayed limber,
> because of the hand of the Mighty One of Jacob,
> because of the Shepherd, the Rock of Israel,
>
> because of your father's God, who helps you,
> because of the Almighty, who blesses you
> with blessings of the skies above,
> blessings of the deep springs below,
> blessings of the breast and womb.
>
> Your father's blessings are greater
> than the blessings of the ancient mountains,
> than the bounty of the age-old hills.
> Let all these rest on the head of Joseph,
> on the brow of the prince among his brothers."
>
> (Genesis 49:22-26 NIV)

In the Bible translation called The Message, the scripture above reads this way:

> *"May they rest on the head of Joseph, on the brow of the one consecrated among his brothers."*

Genesis 48:5-20 reiterates that birth order does not matter, and that birthright and blessings can go to both sons and grandsons. It is God who directs birthright and blessings to His plan. Mission and leadership rests on souls that sing God's song, and blessings flow to those who join His dance of destiny. Did not Judah place Joseph on a road to reach his purpose? Didn't Judah open his eyes to see his sin and make a repentant turn when he realized the grace he had received? God rewarded Joseph with firstborn authority and a double portion... two of the twelve tribes of Israel. He then distributed shared leadership roles to both Ephraim and Judah and

He ensured that blessings of ability, favor, and power would always be available for His purpose.

Joseph's son Ephraim was not his firstborn, but Jacob's hand of favor came to rest on him. Notably, descendants of Ephraim included folks like Joshua and Samuel, who marched to the cadence of God's purpose. From Judah came a king called David and the King of All Kings. A precedent for spiritual sonship is unfolding, and chosen instruments of the Lord are the heirs who will receive birthright and blessings. *Bechora* and *berachot* belong to those who accept God's mission and serve His purpose. The inheritance falls to those who will take on that yoke. It does not belong to those who would act against it. It is for people who will dedicate themselves to building God's family, not necessarily a human being's family.

Joseph's family dumped him in a pit, but he ended up in Egypt to prepare a place for the Hebrews to escape a famine. He prepared the way for them to survive and proliferate. Some years later, Moses' family dropped him in the Nile so that he could float into the job of orchestrating a mass exodus back to the promised land. Both men received a mission and accepted it. Both were given all the resources needed to accomplish it. The wellspring of God's blessing flows to His purpose, and no weapon formed against it stands a chance.

Chapter 5

The Antagonist

Antagonist is a word that means *against*. Anything antagonistic is working against something else. An antagonist is an obvious enemy of another. Interestingly, if we consider medical terminology, it is also a substance that stops the action or effect of another substance.

In Acts 7:22, we see some interesting words.

> *"Moses was educated in all the wisdom of the Egyptians and was powerful in speech and action."*

Those words are so interesting because of these words that we read in Exodus:

> *"But Moses said to God, 'I am nobody. How can I go to the king and bring the Israelites out of Egypt?'"*
>
> (Exodus 3:11 Good News Translation)

> *"Moses objected, 'They won't trust me. They won't listen to a word I say. They're going to say, GOD? Appear to him? Hardly!'"*
>
> (Exodus 4:1 The Message Translation)

> "But Moses pleaded with the LORD, 'O Lord, I'm not very good with words. I never have been, and I'm not now, even though you have spoken to me. I get tongue-tied, and my words get tangled.'"
>
> (Exodus 4:10 NLT)

The facts are that Moses was *indeed* educated in all the wisdom of the Egyptians, and the Egyptians were quite astute in the knowledge of their times. They were well-versed in mathematics, history, medicine, the arts, the physics of work, military strategy, and writing that included hieroglyphs and other written forms. Moses was likely fluent in *at least* three languages (Hebrew, Egyptian, and the trade language called Akkadian). He also would have known about things like laws and treaties, and he probably had experience commanding military units because that skill was a usual expectation for high-born Egyptians.

So, Moses' response to God's call is beyond curious. It is so completely irrational, invalid, bizarre, fallacious, and absurd that we have to wonder about God's reaction to Moses. The Almighty must have thought, *Really? Who do you think made your mouth? (Exodus 4:11) Who made you and directed your every breath and every step of your life and learning up to now? Really? Are you questioning my wisdom and my work in you?*

But even though God must have shaken his head at Moses' reluctance, His thundering message to him was,

> *Just go! I will be with you. I will help you. Just tell them I AM sent you.*

The question that begs to be considered here is:

> *What happened to Moses so, in the moment of God's call, he saw himself as inadequate and incapable?*

Maybe God did not dwell on Moses' reluctance too much because He knew the source of his delusion between the ears. He knew that a certain antagonist was brutally attacking the man He had created. What came out of Moses' mouth was certainly one of the enemy's favorite tricks: *distortion, like mirrors in a fun house,* stirred up in the mind of man. Notice, however, what God does next. He does not strike Moses down. He does not abandon him or look for another guy to do the work. The Mighty One does not stretch forth His hand and shock Moses into truth with a lightning bolt. Instead, He does something simple and amazing. God gives Moses... *a partner.* He sends someone to steady the shaky legs caused by the distortion in his spiritual vision. He provides a co-star for a supporting role in an incredibly important story.

Moses became the third most mentioned character in the Bible, only behind Jesus and David. According to one source, Moses' name appears 803 times in scripture because of his incredible impact in directing God's people. Ponder, then, the outcome if the antagonist in Moses' head had diverted him from his spiritual birthright (*bechora*). Ponder the historical consequences if he had not accepted the mission, taken on the leadership position, and accepted the power God gave as his *berachot* (resources) for the ongoing mission.

A Grand Story Unfolds

In the book of Exodus, Almighty God executed a meticulous plan for a great escape. It was, of course, an escape from captivity. On its face, it was an escape from slavery imposed by Pharaoh. In reality, the captivity was a spiritual reflection of Satan's enslavement that started in the Garden of Eden. God painted a grand picture of the escape route on the screen of human history. Humanity saw a pixel and was clueless about how it fit into the monumental scheme of God's plan. Let's face it: human beings have a carnal intellect and extremely limited vision. That is the unfortunate state of humanity since Satan stepped in, deceived man, and confused things royally.

God took an imperfect man (Moses) and a shepherd's staff (hereafter referred to as *the stick*) and put on, at least for the Old Testament era, the greatest show on earth. He displayed His power against the tricks of Satan so His people could spot the enemy! Think about it. Moses told Aaron to throw a staff on the ground, and it turned into a snake. The magicians and sorcerers of Pharaoh did the same trick. During the first two plagues, Pharaoh's magic guys also turned water into blood and did a *voila* with some frogs. Did you ever wonder why God didn't just start with a power move that Pharaoh's guys couldn't copy?

Is it possible that God wanted to show His Jewish family, starting with Moses and Aaron, that an enemy hovered near who was far more treacherous than Pharaoh? Did He want them to figure out the spiritual force motivating Pharaoh had some power, too? Maybe God wanted his Jewish family to see the nasty enemy among them and know there was trouble ahead. He probably wanted His people to understand there was a fight going on in the spiritual realm and they needed to choose the right side!

When the power contest was over in Egypt, God had spanked the enemy. Pharaoh let the Jews go, but the Hebrews had barely made it out of Egypt before Pharaoh's heart hardened and he chased God's people down. The Jews started wavering and falling apart when the Egyptians showed up. They panicked and asked Moses,

> *"Were there not enough graves in Egypt? Did you have to bring us out here to die?"*

> (Exodus 14:11)

Moses made his first response to their whining:

> *"Do not be afraid. Stand firm and you will see the deliverance the Lord will bring you today; you will never see these Egyptians again. The Lord will fight for you; you need only to be still."*

> (Exodus 14:13-14 NIV)

Right there, Moses propped the Israelites up for the first time.

Listen to the words:

> *"Don't be afraid. Stand firm and you will see…"*

He could have said, "Look Hebrews, if you have just seen the same signs and wonders I just saw and you still can't figure out that God is with you and he will take care of things, then just lay down right here in the road and die." That would have been *rebuke*. However, Moses, at least at that moment, had the composure (and the Holy Help from Almighty God) to say, "*Stand firm. God loves you, and He's got this.*" He knew he needed to put *courage* into them by getting their attention off the Egyptians and getting their focus back on their all-powerful God. Let me repeat that. He needed to get *courage* in them. They needed *encouragement* because courage was absent. Courage left them when doubt, insecurity, a lack of confidence, and *fear* took over. Insecurity gives way to *doubt*, and *doubt* gives birth to uncontrolled *fear*. That's the devil's plan to destroy what God loves: me and you. (Stay tuned for a coming commentary about the word doubt.)

Now *courage* (not letting fear control us) gives birth to *trust*, and *trust* gratified becomes a more fortified *faith*. Moses was "en"couraging the Israelites. He was putting courage *in* them to get them in a position of *trust* so they could learn to have *faith*.

Even after God caused the Red Sea to swallow the Egyptians, Satan attacked the Israelites relentlessly. He used his trademark lies and fear factors to cause them to freak out, grumble, complain, and blame when they did not have water. It was the same song, the second verse, when they did not have food. Then, since Satan had been so successful in making those Hebrews afraid of dying from thirst one time, he tried that tactic once again. *Nice*.

Yes, even then, those Hebrews chose *fear* over *faith*. Why? It was because those humans were affected then, as they are now, by an opposing force. Make no mistake. There *is* an opposing force, and it is every bit as active *now* as it was *then*, trying to snatch what God loves (namely, us!) out of His hands.

"The whole Israelite community set out from the Desert of Sin, traveling from place to place as the LORD commanded. They camped at Rephidim, but there was no water for the people to drink. So they quarreled with Moses and said, 'Give us water to drink.' Moses replied, 'Why do you quarrel with me? Why do you put the LORD to the test?' But the people were thirsty for water there, and they grumbled against Moses. They said, 'Why did you bring us up out of Egypt to make us and our children and livestock die of thirst?' Then Moses cried out to the LORD, 'What am I to do with these people? They are almost ready to stone me.' The LORD answered Moses, 'Go out in front of the people. Take with you some of the elders of Israel and take in your hand the staff with which you struck the Nile and go. I will stand there before you by the rock at Horeb. Strike the rock, and water will come out of it for the people to drink.'

So, Moses did this in the sight of the elders of Israel. And he called the place Massah and Meribah because the Israelites quarreled and because they tested the LORD saying, 'Is the LORD among us or not?'"

(Exodus 17:1-5 NIV)

God did a miracle to make bitter water sweet. He provided quails and manna every day for food. He even quenched their thirst a second time by bringing water out of a rock. Should we also mention those ten plagues, an epic escape from Egypt, and a mass drowning of the enemy when the Hebrews didn't even get muddy? Sadly, they had more to learn about the Almighty. These Hebrews were just not *getting it*.

Certainly, there was much going on in this chapter of Exodus. There was evidence this group of Hebrews had an exceptionally short memory and an exceedingly small tank of faith. They were like toddlers, taking little steps and then tumbling and crashing every time. They did not see all they needed to do was look up to their Father and grab onto His powerful hand. As we look a little closer, though, we can see that Yahweh was always ready to teach the next lesson to these beings, who were pitifully inflicted with the carnal curse. These people suffered from total blindness to the spiritual because they focused on what the flesh wanted most. When the Hebrews were thirsty, for instance, getting something to drink was the carnal desire of the day. They threw a tantrum about water instead of praising God for his care and asking nicely for what they needed.

Notice what God did next. He told Moses to get the stick. The *stick*! This was the object the Hebrews connected to *power*. The one that brought all the plagues upon Egypt. The one that parted the Red Sea and always did what needed doing.

The *stick* might remind some who are a little older than others of when their own little mommas *got the stick* during their childhood years. That *stick* was to give a quick and emphatic reminder of who was in charge and what one needed to do to comply with Mamma's requests. She had the *power* to make a child behave. She was not especially interested if the child wanted to or not.

Remember, however, that even though God also wants compliance, he wants the kind that comes from a genuine place of obedience, reverence, and the freedom to choose. So, when Moses got *the stick*, it was about two things. First, it was a reminder that God can be trusted to meet our needs in all circumstances. God instructed Moses (a leader and example) to use the stick (the symbol of power) to bring water (what was needed) out of a rock (not a usual home for water but certainly a symbol of Christ and the living water he would later bring forth). God displayed His power and nature as Jehovah Jireh (our provider) to overcome the challenges of the flesh that get humans distracted from Yahweh (the name that means *He who causes everything to be*). Father God did not punish the Hebrews and send them to bed hungry. He taught them, stone by stone, who He was and why they should trust him.

Why stone by stone? Well, notice that He brought that needed water out of a stone, and then stay tuned for more:

> *"Then came Amalek and fought with Israel at Rephidim."*
>
> (Exodus 17:8 KJV)

Showdown In the Wilderness

In our earlier examination of the Jacob and Esau story, there was evidence of an antagonist coming against God's mission, His chosen leadership, and the resources that went with it. In the human scene, it was a conflict between two brothers. It seems, however, that there was also a spiritual realm involved that moved the human players toward their actions. Abundantly clear was the fact that in despising his birthright, Esau was not signing up to be God's mission warrior. He was far more interested in the material spoils of the inheritance. The spirit that influenced Esau was not the same spirit that motivated Jacob. It was a spirit antagonistic to God.

As we look at this interesting picture of a key moment in the Bible, it is interesting that Amalek, a direct descendant of Esau, was now attacking Israel. He attacked the Israelites at Rephidim and was now about to engage them in a major battle. Though the fight broke out in the earthly realm, there was a real possibility that something more ominous was taking place in the spiritual realm above the fight.

Remember, Satan often conscripts people to do his evil bidding, so it is profound that Amalek has an incredibly interesting name. In Hebrew, each letter of the alphabet corresponds with a number. Poignantly, the letters in the name Amalek have the same numerical value as the Hebrew word *safek. Safek means doubt.*

There is now something on the battlefield that is a blatant and sinister antagonist to faith.

When the Israelites experienced thirst, they responded with *doubt*. They said, "Is the Lord with us or not?" When we read Exodus 17 verses 7 and 8 together, it is as if the scripture is saying (paraphrase), *When the people questioned God's provision, they complained against Him. Yes, indeed, Amalek (doubt) was attacking them.* Their faith was under attack, and it was being attacked from the vantage point of their immediate weakness. The mention of this story in Deuteronomy adds the details of "when you were tired and weary" to further describe this moment of assault.

So while we read about a physical attack by Amalek, let us also look at the spiritual war and the Lord's response to it. What did Moses do? He fought a spiritual fight with spiritual weapons.

> "Moses said to Joshua, 'Choose us out men, and go out, fight with Amalek: tomorrow I will stand on the top of the hill with the rod of God in my hands.'"

(Exodus 17:9 KJV)

In his hands, Moses held *the stick*. High above the enemy, he held the staff (the symbol of God's power), which had delivered them repeatedly from every kind of trouble. He held it high so all could see it. He made sure it was the point of focus during the conflict. While the Israelites kept their eyes on God and their allegiance fixed firmly on Him, they *prevailed*. There are two spiritual issues displayed in this scene. First, it is always important for God's people to keep their focus on the Almighty, All-Powerful God and not on the problem at hand. Second, there is an enemy who wants to do everything possible to keep humans distracted in the fight so they *cannot* focus on God. Moses' job, in this Biblical moment, was to keep the symbol of God's power in sight and held high over the situation. Notice that Moses stood on a hill. He got as high over the battle as he could climb to get above the conflict. And then *he worshipped*. God's servant held the symbol of God's power high... and *he worshipped*. He declared God's sovereignty over this and all situations. Moses looked up, and he kept his eyes on God and His *power—not* on the problem. So, while he kept his staff held high and his eyes on the Lord, the Israelites prevailed. And who was on the battlefield? It was Joshua, whose name meant "God saves." Joshua was on the battlefield with the *sword*, known also as the *Word* of God, which had already been spoken to say:

> *I AM the one who provides for you. (Exodus 16:13-15)*
>
> *I AM the one who heals you. (Exodus 15:26)*
>
> *I AM the one who saves you (Exodus 14:30)*
>
> *I AM the one who will fight for you. (Exodus 14:25)*

Lo-and-behold, Moses, too, was human and sometimes grew weary. So, Aaron and Hur were on the scene in a critical supporting role. Moses needed support. He needed help. He needed extra strength when his strength was failing. Moses needed the *power of a partner.* So, what did these men do?

First, they supported. They helped Moses stay in worship. More exactly, they helped him keep his eyes on the Lord. They added their strength when Moses' strength was running low, and they added their support in the struggle. They became human vessels for the Holy Spirit, who comes to attend us (often through others) when we are weak.

> *"...the Spirit helps us in our weakness. We do not know what we ought to pray for, but the Spirit himself intercedes for us through wordless groans. And he who searches our hearts knows the mind of the Spirit, because the Spirit intercedes for God's people in accordance with the will of God."*
>
> (Romans 8:26-27 NIV)

Finally, Aaron and Hur also performed another amazing feat. When Moses grew weary and weak, they brought in a rock. In the Bible, a rock is the symbol of steadfastness, strength, and durability (Genesis 49:24; Deuteronomy 32:4; Psalm 18:2; Psalm 18:31). Because this fight would continue for a long time, Moses needed all those things. His two cohorts, Aaron and Hur, needed those things as well, as they intervened to help hold up Moses' arms. They put a *rock* under Moses, and that rock, like the rock that had just poured out water so that the Israelites would live, was *Christ*.

> *"...for they drank from the spiritual rock that accompanied them, and that rock was Christ."*
>
> (I Corinthians 10:4)

Behold the image in Exodus 17:9-13. God's servants are standing in the power of God the Father, God the Son, and God the Holy Spirit, while the *Word* of God does its work.

> *"...so is my word that goes out from my mouth: It will not return to me empty but will accomplish what I desire and achieve the purpose for which I sent it."*
>
> (Isaiah 55:11 NIV)

This is the same God who said:

> *"The Lord will fight for you; you need only to be still."*
> (Have Faith)
>
> (Exodus 14:14 NIV)

In this awe-striking picture, we see Yahweh, the All-Powerful One, who brings into existence anything that exists, God the Holy Spirit (Ruach Elohim), who is the activating power of God's will, and out in that field, the *sword* (God's Word). In this scenario, Amalek is doomed. *Then* and *now*.

And who is Amalek? Well, scripture says he is a descendant of Esau. So were some other Bible notables, like King Agag in the Book of Samuel, Haman in the Book of Esther, and Herod in the Life of Christ. But in the spiritual realm, Amalek is *doubt* and the origin of it. Amalek is a spirit that opposes God, and the direct opposite of *faith*. The spirit of Amalek has conscripted many men to oppose God in diabolical ways. Amalek, throughout the Bible, henceforth, equates to the metaphorical *spirit of evil*. God designates Amalek as *one who raises his hand against God*, and he makes this spiritual declaration:

> *"Then the LORD said to Moses, 'Write this in a book as a memorial and recite it to Joshua, that I will utterly wipe out the memory of Amalek from under heaven.' And Moses built an altar and named it, The Lord Is My Banner; and he said, 'Because the Lord has sworn, the Lord will have war against Amalek from generation to generation.'"*

(Exodus 17:14-16 NASB)

In Deuteronomy, there is another reference to this experience of God's people, and it reads like this:

> *"Remember what Amalek did to you on the way as you were coming out of Egypt, how he met you on the way and attacked your rear ranks, all the stragglers at your rear, when you were tired and weary; and he did not fear God."*

(Deuteronomy 25:17-18 NKJV)

Pay close attention to two things in this passage from the New King James version, and what it says about the attack. First, this translation speaks of Amalek, not the Amalekites. In verse eighteen, it says *he* did not fear God. That hints at the idea that the scripture is talking about a specific entity. Is it possible that God is talking about *Satan*? Could it be supposed that Amalekites, symbolically and spiritually, are people (any people) that Satan conscripts for his purposes? Second, Amalek attacks God's people when they are weak, tired, weary, without energy, or low on spiritual power. *Who* does *that* sound like?

Chapter 6

Attack, Defense, and Holy Inheritance

In our study thus far, there are two ideas about God's redemption plan for man that loom large. First, there is a mission going on in the realm of man. God calls people to carry it out, and all the resources of heaven flow to that effort. There is, if you will, a spiritual *bechora* (mission) accompanied by spiritual *berachot* (resources) given for the proliferation and protection of the mission. These elements connect, and they should prosper together. Second, part of the blessing that goes with the mission is proliferation and protection. That means antagonism and opposition are inevitable!

In Exodus, we encountered the antagonist who came against God's people in the wilderness. Before that discussion, however, we looked at God's servant Moses and the antagonist within him—the one that caused him to question his ability to serve God in the role to which he was called. Many of God's servants in the redemption plan story suffered that kind of enemy assault.

Elijah, for instance, was so affected by the antagonist that in I Kings 19:3-4, he came undone. Discouragement overwhelmed him. His courage was gone. He was exhausted, weary, without energy, and drained of spiritual power. That was the cue for the antagonist to *move in for the kill*, and Elijah did what most people do in such a condition. He left all help behind and went farther into the wilderness of human weakness. He sat down and came apart and he flung his distress at God.

I've had all I can stand! I'm done! I am a dismal failure, so just kill me!

That was how far into the wilderness he went. Never mind that he had, with God's power,

> stopped the rain from falling on the earth,
>
> brought the dead back to life,
>
> brought down God's proof of fire on a bunch of bull at Mount Carmel (I Kings 18:38),
>
> and then brought the rain back to the earth again.

Elijah still looked in a distorted mirror and saw himself as an utter failure.

Fortunately, God did not kill Elijah. God countered the savage attack from the antagonist with everything his servant needed. He cared for him, ministered to him, and lifted his head to take nourishment. God revived and supported Elijah, and He healed him so that the enemy no longer distorted his vision. God gave Elijah rest and physical nourishment, and then He moved his vision from a distorted mirror back to a picture of God's power. In Elijah's case, the picture came in a wind, an earthquake, a fire, and a still small voice.

The antagonist even attacked Jesus. The assault happened in a wilderness, of course, and Jesus' wilderness represented the weakness of the flesh characteristic of humanity. In typical fashion, Jesus' antagonist waited for the right moment. He ambushed Jesus when he was experiencing the fullness of the flesh brought on by a 40-day lack of food. God again sent someone to attend and help. This time, it was a helper known as the *Spirit* who went with Jesus into the wilderness, and it was the Word of God that defended him. After that, angels came and cared for him. In that wilderness, the enemy saw scathing defeat.

Thus far, we have discussed three key biblical figures in God's plan and how the antagonist attacked them. They are the same figures who stood on a mountain at the transfiguration. They represented three distinct parts of God's redemption plan, and they all experienced the wrath of an enemy's opposition to it. Each of them executed crucial parts of God's mission. Each of them was vulnerable as he did the work God gave him. All of them encountered some kind of wilderness, and all of them experienced a need for *help*. Think about it. They all received help. They all received the help that was needed in the right way and at the right time. God said, "I will help you," and He meant it. But often, he sent His help through another. God gave Moses a partner and a physical instrument (the staff) for confidence. For Elijah, God sent an angel to minister to him and give him nourishment. Then, He put on a display of power to fortify him with boldness. Even Jesus had the company of the Holy Spirit to support him, the Word of God to defend him, and angels to meet His human needs.

It is profound to realize that the three key figures we just discussed were each strategically instructed regarding birthright and blessings. More exactly, they were instructed about *bechora* (mission and leadership) and *berachot* (resources for the mission). Each of these men received instruction and afterward delivered instruction to a spiritual progeny that was selected by God Almighty.

God told Moses to pass the torch of leadership (*bechora*) to Joshua, who would later lead the Israelites into the promised land and act with the same power as his mentor. God spoke directly to Joshua about this transition (Joshua 1:1-6), and the Israelites accepted Joshua into the position without question. He inherited abundant resources (*berachot*) to evidence the faithfulness of God in His promises. These included the power and favor of his spiritual father and predecessor, Moses. God directed His mission and resources through His choice. Again, the birthright (inheritance) belongs to the heart that holds God's mission sacred and dear.

> "And the Lord said unto Moses, 'Take thee Joshua the son of Nun, a man in whom is the spirit, and lay thine hand upon him.'"
>
> (Numbers 27:18)

Elijah, too, received specific instructions about who his successor would be. God told him to find Elisha and anoint him for the job. Elisha walked with and learned from his great mentor for several years, so when the time came for God to take Elijah away, he would not let him out of his sight!

Because Elijah understood he was about to be taken, he asked Elisha what he could do for him. Elisha requested only one thing: to receive a double portion of Elijah's spirit.

Elijah told him he had asked for a difficult thing! He was asking for something that was *not* a tangible commodity, and it was *not* something he could give him. Nonetheless, Elijah told Elisha *if* he saw him when he left, his request would be granted. Elisha indeed saw Elijah when he left, and he cried out,

> *"...My father! My father!"*

> (II Kings 2:12)

Elisha's words tell us that Elijah was his *spiritual* father, but a more striking relationship was about to be revealed. God himself had chosen Elijah's spiritual son and appointed him to become the spiritual leader of his legacy. Elisha would continue Elijah's spiritual mission. God had assigned a spiritual "birthright" to a man called Elisha, and a blessing was to follow.

The firstborn son was to receive a *double portion* of his father's wealth, along with the birthright. Though Elisha was a *spiritual* son, he had been specifically given the right of succession by God himself. It was, therefore, right for Elisha to ask for a double portion of the Holy Spirit his "father" possessed. God chose Elisha as Elijah's successor. He also gave His Holy Spirit and the power of it as a *resource* to Elijah, his prophet. Accordingly, Elisha was just asking for his rightful inheritance. It was, however, an intangible gift, and only God could distribute it.

Hold on to these ideas:

- *bechora... berachot*
- God-given mission... God-given resources
- spiritual father... spiritual child
- mentor... mission

The other person at the transfiguration was Jesus. Therefore, we should consider that the very definition of the word *transfigure* is *to transform into something more beautiful and elevated*. Other words for transfigure are *transform, rearrange, and revolutionize*. For our understanding of what Jesus was about to do in God's mission to redeem mankind, those words are *earth-shaking*.

> *"Therefore, there is now no condemnation for those who are in Christ Jesus, because through Christ Jesus the law of the Spirit who gives life has set you free from the law of sin and death. For what the law was powerless to do because it was weakened by the flesh, God did by sending his own Son in the likeness of sinful flesh to be a sin offering. And so he condemned sin in the flesh, in order that the righteous requirement of the law might be fully met in us, who do not live according to the flesh but according to the Spirit."*
>
> (Romans 8:1-4)

> *"For those who are led by the Spirit of God are the children of God. The Spirit you received does not make you slaves, so that you live in fear again; rather, the Spirit you received brought about your adoption to sonship. And by him we cry, "Abba, Father. "The Spirit himself testifies with our spirit that we are God's children. Now if we are children, then we are heirs— heirs of God and co-heirs with Christ, if indeed we*

> *share in his sufferings in order that we may also share in his glory."*

(Romans 8:14-17)

This changes *all*. This *revolutionizes* everything. God has appointed that the birthright and the blessings belong to those whose hearts are turned to Him. They do not belong to birth order, fame, wealth, strength, good looks, nationality, or luck. Again... they belong to the ones whose hearts are turned to God. And that now means those who accept the sacrifice of His son, Jesus Christ, on the cross for the atonement of sins. Along with our salvation comes *inheritance*! When we were born again unto Christ, we received our birthright, our *bechora*. We became *joint heirs* with Christ. We *share* the birthright of Christ. Remember, the firstborn receives birthright, mission, responsibility, and position of authority. Because we are joint heirs, we share responsibility for the family *enterprise* and the family *mission*.

> *"The Spirit himself bears witness with our spirit that we are children of God, and if children, then heirs— heirs of God and fellow heirs with Christ, provided we suffer with him in order that we may also be glorified with him."*

(Romans 8:16-17)

> *"And if you are Christ's, then you are Abraham's offspring, heirs according to promise."*

(Galatians 3:29)

"So you are no longer a slave [to sin], but a son, and if a son, then an heir through God."

(Galatians 4:7)

"For those whom he foreknew he also predestined to be conformed to the image of his Son, in order that he might be the firstborn among many brothers."

(Romans 8:29)

He is the image of the invisible God, the firstborn of all creation."

(Colossians 1:15)

"I pray that the eyes of your heart may be enlightened in order that you may know the hope to which he has called you, the riches of his glorious inheritance in his holy people, and his incomparably great power for us who believe."

(Ephesians 1:18-19)

"For the promise to Abraham and his offspring that he would be heir of the world did not come through the law but through the righteousness of faith."

(Romans 4:13)

We share the inheritance of Christ. We are fellow heirs. However, we need to understand that with the blessings (the resources) we inherit both a mission and a responsibility for leadership. We are to make disciples, teach, and serve.

> *"Then Jesus came to them and said, 'All authority in heaven and on earth has been given to me. Therefore go and make disciples of all nations, baptizing them in the name of the Father and of the Son and of the Holy Spirit, and teaching them to obey everything I have commanded you.'"*
>
> *(Matthew 28:18)*

As fellow heirs, we do not all have the same role or the same gifts, but we are to use what we *receive* for the mission we have been given.

> *"Having gifts that differ according to the grace given to us, let us use them:"*
>
> (Romans 12:6)

We have received gifts, talents, and energies to use in our mission! We also have access to the power and *authority* of Jesus Christ. This last bit of information is essential because, as we pursue our mission, just like Moses, Elijah, and even Jesus, we are likely to encounter *the wilderness* and *the enemy*.

Chapter 7

The Mission Attacked

In II Kings 24, we can read about the Babylonian siege of Jerusalem. As Nebuchadnezzar finished the destruction of this city, his finale was to take away its riches. He seized treasure like gold and silver, of course, but he also carried away people with all kinds of skills and talents. II Kings 24:14 says this:

> *"He carried all Jerusalem into exile: all the officers and fighting men, and all the skilled workers and artisans—a total of ten thousand."*
>
> (II Kings 24:14)

Nebuchadnezzar certainly realized that there are valuable treasures stored in human beings and these particular human treasures ended up in Babylon. Others of God's flock got scattered, too, and ended up on other mountains and hills.

> *"My people are like sheep whose shepherds have let them get lost in the mountains. They have wandered like sheep from one mountain to another, and they have forgotten where their home is."*
>
> (Jeremiah 50:6 Good News Translation)

Truthfully, vast numbers of God's people are "scattered" today, as well. Further, in all the scattered, there are skills, talents, and abilities that could serve as valuable tools in God's mission for His church. In The Purpose Driven Church by Rick Warren, Pastor Warren makes this resonating statement:

"If we can ever awaken and unleash the massive talent, resources, creativity, and energy lying dormant in the typical local church, Christianity will explode with growth at an unprecedented rate."

(The Purpose Driven Church, Grand Rapids: Zondervan, 1995)

Pastor Rick Warren

Satan is using dirty tactics to attack the church today, and one of his favorite strategies is to neutralize and disable its resources. In any war, if one side can disable the weapons and resources of the other side, it gains an advantage.

After Pastor Warren's statement just quoted, he described a Gallup survey showing that the number of American church members who are active in any kind of personal ministry is only 10 percent. Further, 50 percent have no interest in getting involved in any kind of personal ministry, while 40 percent say they 1) have not been asked or 2) do not know how.

Some may read the former data and label the statistic showing only 10% involved in ministry as *apathy*. But could it be that there is a different reason for the lack of involvement in ministry? To that point, here is an interesting question to ponder: If there is a lamp in your home that is not producing light, is it apathetic? We would agree that it is not. It may have a light bulb that is burned out. It may not be plugged in. Possibly, a storm has caused a temporary loss of power. Or maybe the humans in the house just have not used the switch to turn it on.

When the human body is not working as it should, we don't call that apathy. We call it pathology. We look for a cause, and we try to restore function. When the body of Christ is not functioning as *it* should, we also need to look for causes and ways to restore intended performance. We may need to replace something, connect people to power, or flip a switch. If we want to give people in the church the power to fulfill their purposes, judgment just will not work. However, spiritual intervention invites all kinds of possibilities.

Noting that only 10 percent of church members are actively involved in ministry, it certainly sounds like the sheep are scattered, as the scripture says. Worse, those scattered sheep are talented people who hold down jobs, have all kinds of skills and talents, and also have many varieties of education. In a 2020 Gallup Poll, church membership was measured across age groups. The data showed that only 47% of adults in the United States belonged to a church, synagogue, or mosque. Religious membership has dropped from 73 percent to 47% in the last 25 years. Of the 47% who are religiously affiliated, an even lesser number are in the Christian church. And we just mentioned that among members of churches, only 10% engage in active ministry. It sounds like **now** is the ideal time for churches to work toward a spiritual breakthrough.

We are challenged to face the truth. As Christians, we have a *birthright*. We are God's chosen leadership for His mission. We also have our Father's *blessings* and abundant favor, gifts, talents, and energies to empower the mission and make it successful.

> *"...He gives us grace and glory. The LORD will withhold no good thing from those who do what is right.*
>
> (Psalm 84:11 NLT)

God's favor and blessings are bestowed upon those who walk in righteousness. He graciously provides everything necessary for our success and does not withhold any good thing from us.

> *"And God is able to bless you abundantly, so that in all things at all times, having all that you need, you will abound in every good work."*
>
> (II Corinthians 9:8 KJV)

Hence, let us turn our attention back to that meager 10 percent of church folks who are actively involved in mission, to the 40 percent of wannabes, and to the 50 percent that dwell in the spectator seats.

They are very much the focus of this writing because there is compelling evidence that the folks who sit on the sidelines are there because the enemy has diabolically detained them. With a little adjustment, a flip of a switch, or a live connection to power...*that could change*!

Chapter 8

Exposing the Enemy

Before we get powered for purpose, as the title of this book suggests, there are nagging matters we must understand better. The church people we discussed in the last chapter aren't on the sidelines by accident! Satan knows people are most definitely like sheep, and there is hard evidence that he knows exactly how to attack and scatter the flock.

People in churches can become inert. That means they are shut down. They are not functioning as intended. How did they get this way? Well, the enemy has likely unleashed his strategy of removing folks from kingdom work through variations of his favorite strategies, including pain, isolation, distortion, and fear. Recall the biblical moment when Moses could not see his capabilities. Think about how Elijah came undone and fled to the wilderness. Are God's people today any less likely to be targets of Satan's attempts to attack and disable them than these mighty biblical figures? *This book is not about blame. This book is about rescue!* Search and rescue will be easier if we take the time to understand why people sit on the sidelines.

Stay with me while we examine and confront the evidence of enemy strategy at work in our world today. Get ready to look at some weighty social science in this chapter! Just know that the point is not to get lost in facts and statistics. It is to dig into the root of the problem so we can confront it.

How Modern Society Scatters the Sheep

Perhaps more than at any other time in history, we are struggling with societal factors that make us vulnerable to Satan's agenda. Satan likely loves the design of modern life for just that purpose. Cultural changes occur at a rapid pace, creating two conditions very antagonistic to the Christian faith. One is the constant spew of all kinds of information and communication. The other is the increasing isolation of human beings. While these two conditions almost seem opposed to each other, they are ominously linked.

Not so long ago, people lived in communities that included extended family and other people who shared their values. Today, people live in the *community* of the internet. Exposed to a glut of lifestyles, ideas, and values, it becomes difficult to adopt any that are their own. People have social media *friends* and people who *follow* them in artificial representations of themselves, but genuine relationships are often elusive.

Satan has also used the lure of prosperity and progress to deceive us into a societal catastrophe that has separated us from God. In pursuing prosperity, careers, and self-realization, we have lost scores of our most important anchors for whole, purposeful living. We also have lost intrinsic builders of character, capability, mental health, and maturity.

People have traded small communities for large metropolitan areas and higher-paying jobs. Workers are often far away from the actual places of their work. They may commute long distances, or they may work for an entity or organization that is far away and with which they have no personal relationship. People want to live in larger cities for more entertainment options, and they use their resources to secure things that signal more prestige. They often move farther away from extended families and traditional support systems, and they are growing farther away from each other because of their lifestyles and the schedules they keep. Institutions like schools and churches have become bigger and more complex and often create environments of anonymity. More menacing, however, is the fact that both formal media and social media have become enormously bigger and more convoluted in the ways they present reality to us every day.

People in our nation and our world have become greedy, narcissistic, idolatrous, and lost. As individual human beings, we have become *separated, closed, hidden, anxious, lonely, and vulnerable.* We have left ourselves unguarded and set ourselves up to be the easy prey of Satan. We essentially find ourselves in a relational and spiritual wilderness.

If we do not show up for church, no one notices. If we do not get involved, no one notices. If we are sick, struggling, in debt, or suicidal, no one notices that either. We interact in superficial relationships where we do not know each other, and we do not want the people we see every day to know us because we do not want them to see what is going on in our lives. We do not want people to judge us.

Sadly, only a small percentage of people in the United States today are even connected with a Christian church. *Most people are in a bigger sea of humanity and are traveling in a much smaller boat.*

Illness in the Flock

Modern life, although busy and full of interaction with all kinds of people, has eroded *relationships* and produced *isolation*. Further, isolation is not necessarily about being physically away from people. More often, it is about relational *distance*. Whether the distance is self-imposed or a product of societal characteristics, the same effects are produced. If a person is depressed or anxious, he may withdraw and become more isolated. He could also experience loneliness and become depressed and anxious. If a person has experienced trauma or any kind of relational pain, he may experience fear, and fear may cause a person to withdraw emotionally and self-isolate. Similar responses are produced in the brain and body, regardless of which part of the pathology occurred first. Somewhat like the question of which came first, the chicken or the egg, the question of which part of the human pathology came first is pretty much irrelevant. Most relevant is the resulting change in physiological and environmental function. We are focusing on isolation and loneliness because of their co-morbidity with a plethora of symptoms, not only of psychological pathology but also of physiological illness.

We are most definitely like sheep who are scattered and alone. A 2020 survey reported that 36 percent of Americans admit they are lonely. Sixty-one percent of young adults report serious loneliness, and 51 percent of mothers with young children report the same condition. (Loneliness in America: Making Caring Common, Harvard School of Education, 2020.) Other research by Cigna, a national health insurer, also measured the extent of loneliness in the United States. Using the well-validated UCLA loneliness scale, the study found that a high percentage of Americans classified as *lonely*. Though this loneliness assessment establishes a score of 43 as the indicator for significant loneliness, many with higher scores and specific indicators are experiencing even more intense loneliness and social isolation. Here is an enlightening excerpt from an article describing that study.

"More than half of survey respondents — 54 percent — said they always or sometimes feel that no one knows them well. Fifty-six percent reported they sometimes or always felt like the people around them 'are not necessarily with them.' And 2 in 5 felt like 'they lack companionship,' that their 'relationships aren't meaningful' and that they 'are isolated from others.' Members of Generation Z, born between the mid-1990s and the early 2000s, had an overall loneliness score of 48.3. Millennials, just a little bit older, scored 45.3. By comparison, baby boomers scored 42.4. The Greatest Generation, people ages 72 and above, had a score of 38.6 on the loneliness scale."(Chatterlee, 2018)

To summarize, this research renders three specific conclusions:

1. Loneliness is widespread throughout this nation.

2. Loneliness does not necessarily relate to how many people we are around or how *often* we are around people.

3. People in the last four generations have become progressively less effective in the creation and maintenance of satisfying personal relationships.

Another wrinkle in the study of human discomfort is that people frequently do not *know* what is causing them pain. They know they do not feel good, that they don't feel right, or that they somehow are hurting, but they rarely recognize what exactly they are experiencing. That is where the art and the science of asking questions both become pivotal. I will wager right now, with great confidence, that many people who are experiencing loneliness, for instance, cannot identify their state as loneliness. Even those surrounded by people often suffer discomfort. They may have stable marriages and people they call friends, but they are still lonely. Often, the experience of loneliness presents itself as something else, like depression or anxiety. People isolate themselves in some obscure way and increase their pain. Sometimes, pain hovers in the background and people shove it down and deny it. Unfortunately, pain, whether it is loneliness, anxiety, depression, emotional trauma, or constant anguish of any kind, gets between our ears where the enemy can use it against us. When pain drives us into any kind of isolation, monsters of the mind can get bigger, meaner, and far more damaging.

It is also noteworthy that what *produces* scores on the loneliness scale relates more often to *isolation* in various forms. Sometimes people self-isolate for emotional protection. Self-isolation can result from hiding one's *real* self so that another self can be projected. Often, an individual employs this strategy to make himself more acceptable in social situations. And again, multiple aspects of modern society just create a more isolated day-to-day existence.

Now back to the article. Why would an insurance company be studying loneliness, you ask? Well, because it profoundly affects our physical health, our mental health, and how long we live. According to the Health and Medicine Division of the National Academies of Sciences, Engineering, and Medicine, *loneliness* is so detrimental to health that health providers should collect information about social connections and social isolation, along with lifestyle information about diet, exercise, and habits.

Loneliness has a profound effect on the human body and the human brain. Interestingly, scientific research has verified that social isolation and loneliness result in a 29 percent increase in the risk of heart disease and a 32 percent increase in the risk of stroke. Social isolation and loneliness also increase risks of hypertension, diabetes, cognitive decline, and vulnerability to infectious diseases. Research confirms that being objectively isolated, or even having a perception of isolation, can increase inflammation to the same degree as physical inactivity. Further, lower social support is associated with *higher* inflammation and *chronic* inflammation throughout the body and has been linked to various chronic illnesses across the lifespan. These include cardiovascular disease, cancer, diabetes, depression, and Alzheimer's disease. (Our Epidemic of Loneliness and Isolation: The U.S. Surgeon General's Advisory on the Healing Effects of Social Connection and Community, 2023.)

Another interesting fact about loneliness is that it decreases self-regulation. According to VeryWellMind, a mental health and wellness resource staffed by physicians, psychologists, and clinicians, self-regulation is

- the ability to control one's behavior, emotions, and thoughts in pursuit of long-term goals, and

- the ability to manage disruptive emotions and impulses.

Curiously, behavioral scientists have learned that loneliness is *self-perpetuating*. Our thoughts and emotions around loneliness cause us to be hypervigilant in social situations. In simple terms, instead of *what you see is what you get*, it's more like you get whatever you were already perceiving when you walked into a situation. Lonely people stay lonely because they assume that because they are lonely, people don't like them. In social situations, they only gather perceptual information that can support that belief. They leave out other data in their field of experience that is contrary to that assumption. Beyond that, their interactions and behaviors cause them to be perceived as not wanting relationships, so they consequently don't get them.

To get people out of this quandary, it is necessary to interrupt the thought patterns and response patterns that feed the problem. Once a person feels lonely, he may separate from others physically or emotionally, obviously or subtly. This creates isolation, and isolation then causes all the turmoil to go on between the ears. Sadly, that is where Satan can attack us the most viciously.

Satan attacks the lonely. Just like the predator he is, he looks for people who are tired, weary, weak, and separated from the flock. These are Satan's ideal conditions to steal, kill, and destroy. Satan also attacks the helpless. *The next connection here, then, should be that when God's flock, the church, is separated from each other, there is trouble brewing in the spiritual world.* When we are separated, we are lonely. When we are in a state of withdrawal, loneliness, or separation of *any* origin, we are vulnerable to Satan's lies and tricks. Those are the perfect battle conditions for Satan versus the church. If he can paralyze the body with broken, separated parts, Satan is poised to inflict damage. For those of us who are Christians, the takeaway should be that *Satan has effectively used mutations of social isolation for drastic effect.* We have lost our village of people who hold us up. We have strayed away from the safety of our flock, and we are in trouble.

Loud and clear, here is the point. *When Satan isolates people* with societal conditions like pain, brokenness, fear, or any combination of factors, *he can render them inert.* Satan is an expert in producing distortions that cause people to see themselves as powerless and useless, so they flee to the sidelines. He can essentially *freeze* them so that they are useless in the game. And that, my friends, is why the *Barnabas Effect* we are about to explore is so important in today's church.

We will now move from human science to the care that people need to pursue meaningful engagement in their God-given missions. Our focus will shift to the simple, but perfect medicine of the Great Physician, who knows all about what it takes to heal us and make us whole.

Chapter 9

Paralyzed or Powered Up?

"Now there is in Jerusalem near the Sheep Gate a pool, which in Aramaic is called Bethesda and which is surrounded by five covered colonnades. Here a great number of disabled people used to lie—the blind, the lame, the paralyzed. One who was there had been an invalid for thirty-eight years. When Jesus saw him lying there and learned that he had been in this condition for a long time, he asked him, 'Do you want to get well?' Sir, the invalid replied, 'I have no one to help me into the pool when the water is stirred. While I am trying to get in, someone else goes down ahead of me.'"

(John 5:2-7 NIV)

This man saw himself without hope because he was without help. Even though he did not know what he needed was Jesus, he was keenly aware he was in trouble, and it was painful. Have you ever been there? Have you ever been in a life situation where you desperately needed somebody to help you? Most of us have been there because life can disable us in a myriad of miserable ways.

Most folks can recall a time in life when they just could not move. They can remember a personal roadblock that would not allow them to go forward. They were, in some strange way, paralyzed from pursuing life. It may have been the loss of a loved one, a huge financial setback, or a career disaster. It may have been a betrayal by someone they trusted, a trauma of some kind, a life change, a time of loneliness, or a period of unbearable depression. In times like these, it is common to feel both alone and paralyzed. Some may not have even told anyone. Perhaps they held it together at work, church, and other places, but closer relationships suffered. People experience this kind of paralysis all too often.

Personal paralysis happens. Sometimes the worst kind occurs because of constant messages that we do not matter, we are not worthy, or that we can never be enough. We can't see our abilities, or we are afraid to offer them. We may know we are capable, but we feel uninvited. And sometimes our experiences just leave us feeling useless or invisible.

People anywhere and everywhere can become paralyzed. Even smart, successful people who score high on every test, including all the IQ tests, can experience paralysis. Some cannot see their capability when they look in the mirror, and others are so terrified of failure that much of their total potential remains imprisoned.

People in churches are paralyzed, too. Some do not see themselves as capable. Others do not think they have anything to offer. Many do not think people *see* them, and others are terrified of rejection. A variety of perceptions can keep people from pursuing and fulfilling their purposes. Even worse, many, many people do not even know they *have* a God-given purpose. They come every Sunday, but they choose the spectator seats. That's the safest place to be if you are running low on hope and if you are without help.

Hello Satan! There he is again, doing his everyday business of trying to kill, steal, and destroy. Satan is good at all those things, and, unfortunately, he conscripts many human allies to assist in his efforts.

Compare the invalid in John 5:7 with the paralyzed brother in this passage:

> *"And some men were carrying a man on a stretcher who was paralyzed; and they were trying to bring him in and to set him down in front of Him. But when they*

> *did not find any way to bring him in because of the crowd, they went up on the roof and let him down through the tiles with his stretcher, into the middle of the crowd, in front of Jesus. And seeing their faith, He said, 'Friend, your sins are forgiven you.' The scribes and the Pharisees began thinking of the implications, saying, 'Who is this man who speaks blasphemies? Who can forgive sins, except God alone?' But Jesus, aware of their thoughts, responded and said to them, 'Why are you thinking this way in your hearts? Which is easier, to say: 'Your sins are forgiven you,' or to say, 'Get up and walk?' But so that you may know that the Son of Man has authority on earth to forgive sins, He said to the man who was paralyzed, 'I say to you, get up, and pick up your stretcher, and go home.' And immediately he got up before them, and picked up what he had been lying on, and went home glorifying God."*

(Luke 5:18-26 NASB)

A little lifting and a little carrying can be life changing. The friends of this paralyzed man saw something in their friend that needed a touch from Jesus. They moved him from where he *was* to where he could receive that all-important touch, and it made all the difference.

When we read this scripture passage from the Bible, we are likely thinking of illness and infirmity. Physical healing is certainly in the power of Almighty God, but the word that jumps out for attention here is not illness or infirmity. It is *paralyzed*.

Definition:

1. *Complete or partial loss of function, especially when involving motion or sensation in a part of the body.*

2. *Loss of the ability to move.*

3. *A state of powerlessness or incapacity to act.*

(Merriam Webster Dictionary)

Pay attention to the parts of this definition!

- loss of function
- inability to move
- powerlessness
- incapacitation

It is important to think about all these issues, especially when involving a part of the body. What could delight Satan more than making sure the *body* of Christ **loses** part of its *functionality* so that it cannot *move,* experiences a loss of *power,* or becomes *incapacitated*?

Recall, for a moment, the parts of the Holy Trinity. There is the Father, who creates all that is. There is the Son, the Word, who brings the thoughts of the Father into existence. Then there is the *Spirit,* the *power* that activates and effectuates the will of God. The Holy Spirit gets it done. And what did the Father send to the church as Jesus left the earth? He sent the Holy Spirit to dwell in those who are born again so that they can *activate* the will of God as they interact with people.

When we view the Holy Spirit in that way, we recognize that we have now become more than passive recipients of God's grace. We have become catalysts in His formula for saving mankind. A catalyst is an element that *activates* a process or speeds it up. *A catalyst facilitates the release of power to launch the potential of the elements.* Whereas Satan *inhibits,* incapacitates, and *paralyzes* the potential within us, the Holy Spirit gives it effect. But *we,* the body of Christ, can provide the *vessels* through which the *Holy Spirit* delivers. We can deliver the element that *activates* the potential God placed in a person.

Turn on the television, check your social media, talk to a neighbor, or visit a school. In almost every setting, you will find people suffering from anxiety and depression. You will find people struggling with addictions, people victimized by forms of abuse, people who have allowed themselves to be drawn into evil and all varieties of human destruction, and people who have experienced life in ways that have just left them broken. Wherever humans are found, there is struggle, pain, and fear. There is a force acting against people to paralyze, incapacitate, and keep them from their God-given missions. We have defined *paralyze* already. Now let's define the verb incapacitate. This word means to *take away the ability, power, or qualities that provide the capacity to do something*. Satan obviously wants to stop us from doing something. What does he want to keep us from doing? *He wants to keep us from our mission of glorifying God with our lives.*

Jesus came to *fix* people because people are broken in lots of ways. He would say things like *your sins are forgiven* interchangeably with *get up and walk*. When asked why he ate with tax collectors and sinners, Jesus said,

> "It is not the healthy who need a doctor, but the sick..."
>
> (Luke 5:31-32 NIV)

Emphatically, Jesus was trying to free people from what was keeping them from their God-given missions.

Something jumped out at me one day when I was reading Mark 1:29-31. Here is the passage I was reading:

> *"And immediately he left the synagogue and entered the house of Simon and Andrew, with James and John. Now Simon's mother-in-law lay ill with a fever, and immediately they told him about her. And he came*

and took her by the hand and lifted her up, and the fever left her, and she began to serve them."

Sometimes scripture shouts at us to help us understand, and *this* is what jumped up and flagged me down:

And he took her by the hand and lifted her up, ...and she began to serve...

He took her by the hand!

He lifted her up!

And she began *to serve.*

It occurs to me that Jesus *touched* someone. He gave her his hand, and he lifted her out of the state she was in. And—wait for it—she was no longer incapacitated! She could do something. Suddenly she was capable, and she could engage in a mission.

What, my friends, could happen if we could *touch people, take their hands,* and *lift them up* in such a way that we could *fix* them? What if we could *fix* them so that they could pursue their God-given missions? Guess what Jesus did one Sabbath day? He did something unexpected *in church*! A guy with a shriveled hand was there, and Jesus said,

> "Stretch out your hand."

> (Luke 6:10)

Jesus got him to *stretch,* and suddenly, his hand was restored! Did you see the words? Jesus got the guy to *stretch*, and his *hand* was suddenly *capable* again. It was restored to usefulness. Look back at the man who was lowered through the roof to Jesus. In the NASB and the King James Versions, verse 25 says that when Jesus freed the man from his paralysis, he picked up his mat and went home *glorifying God.* How do we glorify God? We embrace our God-given mission. Further, *we all have one.* Folks, how many people around us are paralyzed or incapacitated and who are not accomplishing their God-given missions? I propose that number would astound you!

When we have turmoil and pain going on in our hearts or our heads, Satan uses isolation, loneliness, insecurity, and separation to attack, disparage, and destroy. He uses these tactics to take us out of the game and end our productivity toward our life's mission. Satan's campaign even strives to destroy our trust in the very people who could help us and heal us. Ultimately, he wants to destroy our faith and our relationship with God, which gives him victory in stealing what belongs to God. But wait! Consider the *or* in the title of this chapter. Instead of being paralyzed, what if people were suddenly *powered up*? What if they were like the paralyzed guy *after* Jesus healed him or like Peter's mother-in-law *after* Jesus healed her? What if they were like the guy who stretched his hand and suddenly realized it had *power* to play?

Chapter 10

The Essence of the Barnabas Effect

God meticulously chose individuals with essential attributes and gifts to launch his early church. Each of these human beings modeled critical elements that the future church would need to emulate so that it could survive and thrive. We could examine the lives of Paul or Peter, for instance, and illuminate traits in them that would edify, strengthen, and grow Christ's church. But here, our focus will be on one man the Bible mentions only 28 times. In this study, we will pursue the good apostle Barnabas.

Ponder these questions. How would the story be different if Barnabas had not promoted Saul to the early church leaders? What if he had not convinced them he had something to offer? What if no Barnabas had stepped in to salvage John Mark's ministry when Paul wanted to ditch him? Without doubt, the absence of Barnabas would have resulted in a substantial loss to the early church. At the very least, there would have been a delay in using some human capital God had earmarked for His purposes. Fortunately, God left nothing to chance. He commissioned a humble servant we know as Barnabas to ensure individuals of His choosing stayed on track.

God calls people to serve in the ways he has gifted them. Unfortunately, the world around those people often presents roadblocks to service. When opposition, delay, discouragement, or other difficulties show up, a mission gets harder. Think about this. If obstacles and discouragement had thwarted Paul's service, his leadership and development savvy could have been applied in many other places. John Mark, too, had many capabilities. He was well-educated, and he had valuable skills, including interpreting and writing. Cut from the missionary team, his education and experience could have been applied in other settings as well. Both these men could have used their talents for something other than evangelism. Both could have been diverted by all the difficult human circumstances around them.

But God not only ordains His work. He also *establishes* it. God provided insurance against the loss of talent to other places in the world because He did not want these human treasures to get scattered among other hills and forget where their home was. God intended for these human assets to land strategically in the service of the early church, and He wanted their gifts and talents to be captured and cultivated for His kingdom mission. Therefore, he ordained a special human instrument to be a partner to others and a vital source of both fortification and encouragement. God called— *a Barnabas.*

In this writing, we will explore the power of *strategic encouragement* and how God wants us to use that tool in His service. There is a desperate need among God's people today for the same spiritual fortification and encouragement needed in the early church. Countless Christians with innumerable gifts and talents are displaced from their true purposes or they fall latent in accomplishing them. More ominously, unthinkable numbers of others have never even met the God who designed them and gave them their beautiful gifts. It is no stretch of the truth to state that perhaps the greatest mission of the contemporary church is to take back what Satan wants to plunder. Thankfully, retrieval *is* possible with the cache of wisdom God has provided in His Word.

Faced with such a monumental challenge, we should remember this:

> *Mammoth foes often fall with small weapons.*

Didn't David conquer a giant with a little stone? Little weapons backed by mighty power are formidable. So let's move forward to examine some mighty little weapons that were hidden purposefully in a partner of biblical proportion.

Discovering Barnabas

As we consider the apostle Barnabas, we find a unique individual who provides a subtle but extraordinary example. This apostle is not like the other apostles. He is not an attention-getter. Barnabas is not flamboyant in preaching, admonishing, writing, or drawing focus to his contributions. This man is not a headliner. He is an understated substance. He is not a flashy vehicle. He is fuel.

Let's now dig into what we are labeling the *Barnabas Effect*. Consider this verse.

> *"Joseph, a Levite from Cyprus, whom the apostles called Barnabas (which means 'son of encouragement'), sold a field he owned and brought the money and put it at the apostles' feet."*
>
> (Acts 4:36-37)

This verse gives us enough information to discover the idea that Barnabas must have been an *all-in* kind of guy. He sold his property and laid it at the apostles' feet with complete, joyous abandon. He held nothing back. Interestingly, the next story in Acts is about Ananias and his wife, who held money back from the group and lied about it. The two stories were perhaps told in proximity to each other to create a purposeful comparison between Ananias and his wife and the apostle Barnabas, who gave what he had honestly and with a willing heart.

Barnabas invested in others with the wealth he had. However, I expect his financial investment was only one reason others wanted this guy on their team. Yes, Barnabas entrusted material wealth to them with a joyful attitude, and by doing so, he probably made the folks around him feel worthy, important, and valued. However, as the moniker *son of encouragement* suggests, there were other kinds of wealth in the character of Barnabas that achieved the same end. Though we have already explored some qualities in the active character of Barnabas, we want to stop here and highlight one that is powerful.

> *"Barnabas was a good man, full of the Holy Spirit and full of faith."*
>
> (Acts 11:22)

That is the essence of the Barnabas Effect. He was full of goodness, full of

faith in God,

faith in people,

faith in what God can *produce* in people,

and full of the Holy Spirit, sent to *walk along* and *beside* people, to fight the forces of darkness that come *against* people when they are trying to walk with the Lord. Here is another glimpse of the Barnabas Effect in action:

> *"But Barnabas took him and brought him to the apostles. He told them how Saul on his journey had seen the Lord and that the Lord had spoken to him, and how in Damascus, he had preached fearlessly in the name of Jesus."*
>
> (Acts 9:27 NIV)

The Bible translation called The Voice says it this way:

> *"Only one person accepted Saul as a genuine disciple, Barnabas, who became Saul's advocate to the apostles. He told the whole story of what happened in Damascus, from Saul's vision and message from the Lord to his transformation into a confident proclaimer of the name of Jesus."*
>
> (Acts 9:27 The Voice)

Barnabas truly listened on many levels. First, he responded to Saul's emotional state. He discerned Saul was no longer *angry* that Christians were opposing the law. Instead, Barnabas detected Saul was fervent with the love of Christ and completely focused on telling people the earth-shaking news of the gospel. Barnabas perceived a distinct transition from arrogance to genuine *humility*. Further, Barnabas was likely the ideal person to evaluate Saul's sincerity.

According to a scholarly article about the character of Barnabas (Robin Branch, 2013), extracanonical stories say that Barnabas was a student of Gamaliel in his youth and that during the time he spent studying with Gamaliel, he also knew a younger student named Saul. Easton's Bible Dictionary (London: T. Nelson and Sons, 1897) also says that Barnabas and Saul were likely schoolmates at the feet of Gamaliel. Verified by the apostle Paul's own words in Acts 22:3, Paul indeed studied in the Temple and was a student of Gamaliel in his growing-up years.

> *"I am a Jew, born in Tarsus of Cilicia, but brought up in this city. I studied under Gamaliel and was thoroughly trained in the law of our ancestors. I was just as zealous for God as any of you are today."*
>
> (Acts 22:3 NIV)

It is certainly possible, then, that Barnabas and Saul knew each other as youths because of their cultural influences. They both lived outside Judea for portions of their lives and spoke fluent Greek as a second language. Advanced education was traditional in the families of both young men and would have included the study of Torah, Jewish History, Halakha, and scriptural interpretation. This formal education usually began between the ages of thirteen and fifteen and would have taken place in Jerusalem. Although the exact birthdates of Saul and Barnabas are unknown, scholars believe both were similar in age to Jesus, and this would make it entirely possible that Saul and Barnabas knew each other during their time of study with Gamaliel.

Extracanonical writings of the New Testament period also suggest that Barnabas was disturbed when he realized his former schoolmate, Saul, was persecuting Christians. Scholars have even put forth the idea that Barnabas tried to plead with Saul to stop the persecution. Indeed, Barnabas could have been the person who first told Saul about the salvation that had come through Jesus, even before Saul had his encounter with the Lord on the Road to Damascus. Most would agree that, if this speculation holds true, Barnabas was a gutsy guy. It would have taken great courage to approach a man who might have killed him just for being a follower of Christ.

Yes, Barnabas possibly had the advantage of longevity in his relationship with Saul. But, more importantly, Barnabas had his own spiritual experience to use as a comparative gauge for understanding Saul's Damascus Road encounter, and he had that critical element of the Holy Spirit within him to aid his discernment. Barnabas was *full of the Holy Spirit*, and the Bible says that the Holy Spirit is the giver of all gifts, including the gift of discernment. John 14:26 says that the Holy Spirit is the one who will "teach you all things," and Barnabas had given the Holy Spirit full permission in his life to do just that. The Holy Spirit is also the part of the Trinity that activates the will of God. Barnabas had given the Holy Spirit complete authority to *use him*. Through the Holy Spirit, Barnabas had the perfect tools inside him to determine the sincerity of this new convert.

An aside: Scientists will tell you that human beings cannot measure anything perfectly. They support this statement by explaining that no tool for measurement can achieve absolute consistency, and that even if a tool could be manufactured flawlessly, humans cannot read measurements with perfect precision. If that is true when humans are measuring in the worlds of chemistry, physics, astronomy, and other sciences, how much more difficult is it to measure emotional or intentional constructs in human beings? How do you measure honesty, sincerity, intent, passion, determination, or motive?

Take note: God *is* truth. He *is* the measurement standard. God sends us the Holy Spirit to give us discernment, understanding and power not available to us through our frail human intellect. He *empowers* us to be instruments in the activation of His plan. In Barnabas, we see a man who had given the Holy Spirit full reign to use him in specific, strategic ways.

Once Barnabas saw the heart of Saul through the eyes of the Holy Spirit, he threw himself into implementing God's plan for his brother in Christ. He started by working to remove obstacles to the mission and purpose God had for Saul.

> *"When he came to Jerusalem, he tried to join the disciples, but they were all afraid of him, not believing that he really was a disciple."*
>
> (Acts 9:26 NIV)

Notice that Barnabas did not just say, "Okay, buddy! Sounds good to me! Good luck out there!" Instead, he *came alongside* Saul, and he moved him along a path to create a situation where Saul could launch his destiny.

He supported Paul with the message that he genuinely believed in him, and he found people who could connect him to specific mission tasks. Barnabas showed his faith in Saul by putting himself on the line with the strategic apostles. He *advocated* for Saul by explaining to others what he had seen, and he gave *evidence* of Saul's sincerity by communicating what he had observed. Barnabas not only said, "I'll vouch for this guy," he said, "I'll walk with him." He committed himself to investing time, effort, friendship, and love into this human being because he believed God loved Saul, and he knew God had a plan to use him.

The scripture is clear that God "set apart" both Saul and Barnabas.

> *"While they were worshiping the Lord and fasting, the Holy Spirit said, 'Set apart for me Barnabas and Saul for the work to which I have called them.'"*

(Acts 13:2 NIV)

It also reveals how both men were to serve different purposes and model different essential charismata in the building of an infant church. God's chosen instruments ignited a synergy of purpose destined to thrive forever. *It will*...through folks like me and you.

Chapter 11

The Barnabas Effect in Action

In the following passage of scripture, we see another powerful example of the Barnabas Effect at work in God's plan:

> *"Some days later, Paul proposed another journey to Barnabas. 'Let's return and visit the believers in each city where we preached the Lord's message last time to see how they're doing.' Barnabas agreed and wanted to bring John Mark along, but Paul felt that was a mistake since John Mark had abandoned them in Pamphylia and hadn't finished the previous mission. Their difference of opinion was so heated that they decided not to work together anymore. Barnabas took John Mark and sailed to Cyprus, while Paul chose Silas as his companion."*
>
> (Acts 15:36-41 The Voice Translation)

Paul looked at the evidence and decided that John Mark was not apostle material. He had failed to meet his (Paul's, not God's) expectations, and so he was not the right person for the venture Paul had in mind. Barnabas, on the other hand, *"took John Mark and sailed."*

Barnabas did for John Mark exactly what he had done for Saul at an earlier time and place. He vouched for him. With the help of the Holy Spirit, he perceived God wanted to use John Mark, and once again, he said, "Because I believe in what I perceive in him, I'll vouch for him." He also said, "I will walk with him."

As an educator, I hear Acts 15:36-39 like this:

Paul used a specific rubric of his own design as a standardized measure to decide if John Mark met the criteria for the program (probably the spiritually gifted program), and when the numbers from his arbitrarily designed measurement tool did not produce the expected score, John Mark was cut from the list. And just to make sure that everyone could feel good about the accuracy of the assessment, Paul added anecdotal, observation-based measures:

"This guy does not complete work as assigned."

Barnabas used a completely different approach. He did not evaluate. He did not create measurement tools and use them to make judgments or sort people into categories based on arbitrary measures of their current level of observable achievement. Barnabas was not an educator. Barnabas was a *miner*. He just saw a little glimmer of something shiny on the surface of a person and knew in his gut that there had to be something valuable in there somewhere.

Miners mine in many places using many methods. Some miners see a plant and wonder what treasures it hides. Is it edible? Can it cure diseases, ease pain, provide fuel or prevent insects from destroying crops? Some miners might see a rock and wonder if it is useful for construction material. Other miners might wonder what minerals it holds, how the minerals might be helpful, or if anything is hiding inside the rock that could have value. Does the rock contain gold, silver or uranium?

Maybe you remember reading about George Washington Carver, who mined things like flour, vinegar, stains, dyes, paints, and writing ink from plants like potatoes and peanuts. Or maybe you know about other historical characters who did a little thinking and said things like, "Whoa! That lightning packs a punch! It must be good for something!" And then some people look at other *people* and wonder:

What's in this person?

What kind of potential is in this human raw material, and what does God want to do with it?

I am sure there are great inventors, scientists, writers, and others who were once kids in a classroom and heard things like, "Stop daydreaming and finish this review. We are about to take a standardized test, and if you don't answer these forty-two questions correctly (out of all the billions and zillions of questions in the world),

you won't pass the test,

you will fail this grade,

you will drop out of school,

and *then* you will never amount to anything!"

Now stop right there and ask yourself a question—the best question. Even if these great inventors, scientists, and writers were in classrooms and somehow had not met all the criteria for workplace readiness as prescribed by their local educational institution and the state education agency, and even if they didn't turn in all the assignments—

How did they make their contributions?

Here is my theory: I am convinced that they were somehow affected, at some point in time, by the *Barnabas Effect*.

Remember those few but important words in scripture that described Barnabas? He was:

- A *Levite*.

By birth into his lineage, he was set apart. He was born to be someone who serves in a *supportive* ministry. You might even say that, as a Levite, he was to be a *facilitator* in the service of God and man.

- His name meant *encourager*.

His name did not mean teacher, evaluator, admonisher, judge, jury, imparter of knowledge, or boss. It meant *encourager*. An encourager puts courage in others. An encourager sees a spark and determines that he will fan it into a flame.

- He was an *investor*.

He invested time, effort, money, heart, and soul into other people and into the work the Lord had assigned him.

- He was an *advocate*.

He supported and encouraged those who needed to be seen and heard. He transported people into a position where they could become potent and have real effect.

To great advantage, Barnabas came alongside Saul and advocated for him with the apostles. He vouched for him. He negotiated an opportunity for him so that others could see and believe how God had changed Saul and anointed him for His work.

He was also a *miner*. He saw potential in people like John Mark, and he believed that by using his God-given gifts faithfully, he could help other people discover the unique gifts and powers *they* had for glorifying God in kingdom work.

(Here is an interesting aside: Did you know the region called Cyprus, from which Barnabas came, had an international reputation for mining?)

As it says in scripture, God set Barnabas apart. He set Barnabas apart because he had something in his spirit that was desperately needed in the work of bringing people to Christ, helping them to walk in faith, and helping them to find personal missions in the service of their Lord. This apostle is not heralded as much as others, but the substance of this man has always been a critical component in keeping the church of our Lord afloat.

Could we grab that term *afloat* for a minute? Perhaps you remember a time when you could not swim, or even a time when you could, but you just needed to keep from going under the water. Likely, you found and used a type of flotation device. Maybe it was a pair of floaties or an air mattress. In either of these cases, you were benefiting from what was inside these devices—air. You could trust the device because of the *buoyant* quality of the air inside it. In the same way, Barnabas held many people up. He probably did not look any different from other people, but somehow, what was in him held people up. It caused them to trust, to try, to revive, to give of themselves, and to find their missions.

What we want to connect with in this book is *that* quality. You might say that we are trying to discover how to provide *spiritual buoyancy* to people who are drowning in a sea of modern society that includes all the tricks Satan has developed to make it so dangerous. God's Word is our *lifeline, and it's time to reach out and grab on.*

Chapter 12

One More Time, With Purpose

Are you interested in hearing about a health intervention that reduces the risk of Alzheimer's by 2.4-fold? Would you be excited to learn that the same intervention would also reduce the risk of macroscopic stroke by 50 percent and the risk of sleep disturbance by 16 percent? Wouldn't it be encouraging to know that there is something that could reduce the risk of cardiovascular disease, diabetes, inflammatory conditions, and even mood and stress disorders so that it effectively lowers the risk of mortality by a whopping 57 percent? According to Majid Fotuhi, MD, PhD, and colleague Sara Mehr (Practical Neurology, September 15, 2015), there is a therapy that will produce all these positive results. It is labelled with a single word, and it is both easy to spell and easy to pronounce. This amazing medicine... is *purpose*.

....

I recently read the following scripture and *saw* it for the first time, even though I guess I had read it many times, maybe with my brain on autopilot.

> "Then some Jews came from Antioch and Iconium and won the crowd over. They stoned Paul and dragged him outside the city, thinking he was dead. But after the disciples had gathered around him, he got up and went back into the city. The next day he and Barnabas left for Derbe."
>
> (Acts 14:19-20)

Paul had taken a beating with rocks! Paul had gone down for the count, and it looked like he was a goner. *But people like Barnabas, who were full of the Holy Spirit, gathered around him.* Did you get that? People locked him up in a spiritual group hug. They showed up for him, stayed with him, and they asked God to use them as vessels of resurrecting love.

Let's face it. Most of us have been clocked by the world before. Something has zapped us, knocked the wind out of us, immobilized us, paralyzed us, or killed our engines. I know I have had many of those moments, and I suspect you have, too. Did people gather around you? Did their love resurrect you? Or did you find yourself abandoned and alone?

Paul was fortunate. He had access to the Barnabas Effect. And the result?

> *"... he got up and went into the city. The next day he and Barnabas went off to Derbe."*
>
> (Acts 14:20)

The result was that Paul got back on his feet and continued to pursue his *God-given purpose*.

Now *there* is an important word: *purpose*. God gives it to each of us to further His kingdom, and he attaches *joy* to it. Satan tries his best to thwart it, destroy it, prohibit it, and rob us of any resources that support it. Why? Because it's that important. Satan lives to obstruct God's plan, and every time he keeps one of God's children from accomplishing his God-given purpose, he enjoys a sinister little victory.

Purpose is the *potion* that keeps us thriving in our lives. Purpose drives us physically, mentally, and *spiritually*.

••••••••••••••

This author spent many years as a school counselor. To work in that field, I studied psychological theories and methodologies and tried to find relevant and practical applications for these in my work. It is hard to keep all those theories, applications, and techniques straight. However, there was one therapeutic approach that reached out and grabbed me. I latched on to it early, and I have never forgotten it because it made perfect sense to me. What I observed in working with children was that techniques often produced only short-term results. In contrast, there was a singular *applied theory* that I knew I could trust to deliver actual change, healing, and long-term results almost every time. It got my attention early because I realized the theory summarized what had set me back on my *own* feet many, many times! It amounts to this: *finding meaning in the muck*.

Theories sometimes get covered up with the dust of everyday footwork. However, I tried hard to *make a difference* with the kids I served. In my efforts, I found that no matter what you want kids to do, whether it is learning information, developing a skill, or adopting productive behaviors, the way to get the job done is to attach meaning to it. *Meaning* makes the magic because, as God-created humans, we are built for meaning. Incidentally, *meaning* produces *mission*. Everything else (learning, gaining skills, work, creativity, problem-solving, you name it) just becomes a necessary step to complete the mission created by the meaning.

So, may I please take you on a brief side trip? We have already explored pathology in today's world and how Satan is using it against God's mission for His people. We are learning about the perfect medicine of the Great Physician and in the first paragraph above we talked about how our physiological health is enhanced and fortified with *purpose*. Now I want to introduce you to Victor Frankl, the *meaning* guy in psychology. This gentleman clearly understood the significance of meaning and purpose, and he knew the importance of getting people connected to that power. Here, we explore his contributions because they bring forth the motivation and spirit of a modern-day Barnabas. Victor Frankl was an Austrian-born Jewish psychiatrist. In 1944, he was captured and taken to Nazi concentration camps in Auschwitz, where he lost his entire family in the Holocaust. He survived, but he credits his survival to his determination to rewrite an important manuscript the Nazis stripped from his possession as he entered the concentration camps. Frankl had to live out the concepts he described in that writing to survive. Subsequently, he had to reconstruct his theory through the lens of his own experience. To understand the uniqueness and power of Frankl's work, a brief comparison to two other prominent mental health moguls may be helpful.

First, Brother Freud said mental health is about the *"will to pleasure."* In his approach, finding out who or what is preventing happiness is important, and blame goes mostly to relationships. Then there is Brother Adler, who said mental health is about power and who and what is taking it away. He made outstanding points about how humans need to feel valued, significant, and competent. He also recognized people need more encouragement and less discouragement. According to Adler, people are mentally healthy when they:

- connect to others
- develop themselves fully, and
- contribute to the welfare of others

He made this profoundly interesting statement:

"Meanings are not determined by situations, but we determine ourselves by the meanings we give situations."

(Alfred Adler)

Frankl, though, is a whole different thinker. First, he throws out the blame game altogether. He says human effectiveness requires the ability to *respond* to what we experience. His primary assumption is that humans need to achieve *meaning* through *responsibility*, and when people are suffering in their mental health, it is because they get trapped in thinking that sends them running around in useless circles. People turn inward, where they (and don't forget Satan) start an internal thought pattern that is self-centered and unproductive. Frankl believed that healing comes when we stop looking inward and backward and ask the questions that matter. Questions like "What is the meaning of your life?" and "What are you doing to fulfill it?" produce thoughts that are far more positive and restorative. Instead of asking who or what is to *blame*, Frankl believed mental health requires moving our energy to the present and the future. He said broken thinking doesn't fix broken people.

Didn't the Bible mention that?

> *"As a man thinketh in his heart, so is he."*
>
> (Proverbs 23:7)

An aside: When I typed that quote from Proverbs, I made a typographical error. I looked back at my page, and it said,

> "As a man thinketh in his *hurt*, so is he."

I will throw it out there that my typing error is also true! Dr. Frankl maintains that meaning and purpose are the *primary* drives of human beings. Pay attention to that! *Meaning and purpose are most important in a person's life!* He also states something else that is profound. He says that for each person, the meaning of life is *unique and specific*, and "it can and must be fulfilled by him alone." Frankl knew that, at the core of human existence, every person needs meaning, not gratification. He said happiness is not the goal of life. It is a by-product. *Meaning* is the goal of life, and people must accept responsibility to find their meaning and live it out. It sounds like he is saying, "Hey, if you want to be healthy, lose your *self* and find your meaning." Didn't the Bible say that, too?

> *"Then Jesus said to His disciples, 'If anyone desires to come after Me, let him deny himself, and take up his cross, and follow Me. For whoever desires to save his life will lose it, but whoever loses his life for My sake will find it. For what profit is it to a man if he gains the whole world, and loses his own soul? Or what will a man give in exchange for his soul?'"*
>
> (Matthew 16:24-26 NKJV)

As we leave this brief study of Frankl psychology, I will insert a personal side note. For sure, in all the work I did in trying to serve children, I learned that talking to children about their immediate circumstances, feelings, and choices was only somewhat effective. Worse, even the best results were often only short-term. However, when I could create a situation where a child knew I *saw* him or her and where I could subsequently get that child involved in a task or a mission that 1) had meaning and 2) connected him to others, I could make a dramatic difference in that child's life. Once I learned that, I was less interested in managing momentary behavior. It hit me that behavior management was about making things work for the teacher and the institution, and, while that was a reasonable goal, the most effective goal was moving the student to a place of meaning and purpose. Connection to meaning and purpose produced something with broader, more far-reaching implications. Working *for* something and *toward* something is incredibly more powerful than working *on* something.

However, there were specific steps after the ones I just mentioned. The entire sequence of working with kids, for me, included observing kids, telling them about what important qualities I saw in them, and then inviting them into something like a leadership opportunity, a learning opportunity, or maybe a competition opportunity. It was always important to get each kid connected to a group of other kids and to make sure that he got the message that he was a crucial, important part of the group. The next steps included staying beside kids and getting them focused on and excited about a mission. I fully understood that *walking beside them* was critical to success. *Being there* to process with them, encourage them, problem-solve with them, and connect them to resources (including other human resources) was essential. The process was about striving with them, hoping with them, struggling with them, celebrating with them, and even sometimes lamenting a little with them. We did not always find success, and we sometimes didn't finish all we had planned. We *did,* however, always construct a *mission,* learn, grow, and connect to other people in meaningful ways. Joyfully, I got to see kids leave my realm of education and continue to use skills, be productive, and achieve success as they moved to new missions in their lives.

What did I just say? It is important to *see* someone. You need to see something shiny in him, even if it is embedded in some rocks and clods. Next, you help him find a mission. Then, you connect him to others who share the mission and/or who can help him with the mission. Finally, you stay with the person, walk beside that person, encourage that person, and stand there like a rock under his feet until he gains legs of his own and can do the same for others.

And there it is. That, my friends, is another glimpse of the Barnabas Effect. *That* is another bit of what I believe we can apply as Christians who want to help others find and fulfill their *God-given purpose.*

Chapter 13

Strategic Power of the Barnabas Effect

I am convinced that Satan's favorite playground is that vast space between our ears. In that place, there are no boundaries, and absolutely anything can become distorted to his specifications. It can be dark in there, and, to Satan, darkness is ideal because darkness has the power to magnify any little thought into a monster. It can turn any little rattling into an avalanche of destruction. *Darkness and isolation* are the conditions needed for Satan to do his destructive *dirty work* effectively. Between the ears is the perfect place for that. So, what is the antidote for darkness and isolation? Obviously, the opposite of darkness is light. *Light* is synonymous with truth. Truth is the *Word of God,* and the *Word* is one with *Jesus.* If we want to get light in our heads, we simply must get Jesus in there. We absolutely *must* get the *Word* in there. And it never hurts, either, if we can manage to "open a window" with some genuine relationship.

What, then, about this thing called *isolation*? We know what that means. It means alone, separated, and confined. So, what is the *opposite* of isolated? It turns out that this question is an interesting and enlightening study that can point us directly to strategic Barnabas behavior. Here are some opposites and near opposites listed by Merriam-Webster:

- accompanied
- chaperoned
- escorted
- adjoined
- flanked
- attached
- coupled
- linked

Here are some of my favorites: *integrated, connected, and liberated*. My all-time favorite word, however, related to the exact opposite of isolated, is the word *flanked*.

Flanked is a word that is incredibly interesting and revealing. Traditionally a military term, it means to protect on all sides. Something is inside the flanks and surrounded for protection. For instance, people flank other people to shield and defend. In a spiritual application, people should surround other people and use love and light to guard against the darkness that wants to take root between their ears. Flanking is a component of relational buoyancy in the sea of human distress. Remember? We spoke of buoyancy (keeping someone afloat) a few pages back.

Consider the word *integrated*. The opposite of isolated, it sounds like it might mean being brought into and made a part of a group. It suggests that someone is being *accepted* into a flock. It implies that other people might see a person as a fellow sheep instead of a wolf, a turtle, a donkey, or a slug. First, they must *see* him at all. Then, they must act on the fact that he needs to be incorporated into a mixture of beings intended for usefulness.

Connected is a term that implies contact. For people to be connected, they must *touch* each other, and it is not physical touch that is needed. It is the deliberate decision of people to give attention, time, and effort to a *relationship*. One can stand in the same line as other people but never connect. Being in the same line with someone or being aware that other human beings are in one's visual or spatial field does not create a connection. Connection requires active attention, time, and effort. The statement that Joe is in your Sunday school class does not connect you to Joe. An announcement to the church that there is a new mission group starting does not connect Joe with the church or the mission, either.

Liberated is quite an interesting opposite of isolated. It suggests that isolated means imprisoned, or at least shackled. Isolation implies that something is preventing a person from moving about or acting freely in the world. Perhaps a situation or perception keeps the person trapped, and he is just in need of a miner to come along and free him to reach his potential.

Accompanied, chaperoned, and escorted are impactful words as well, because they suggest how other people can strengthen fellow travelers. As we delve into targeted Barnabas behaviors in later chapters, these concepts will provide powerful tools for moving people into both spiritual confidence and personal mission.

Maybe when people are isolated and struggling with darkness and discomfort between their ears, they need a Barnabas. Isn't it true that the nature of a Barnabas is to come alongside a person, to flank that person, to walk *with* him, and not just notice that he exists? A Barnabas can connect a person with his mission! A Barnabas can be the exact instrument that *facilitates* another person's opportunity to experience joyful obedience to God's plan for him.

Let's face it. Life often wears on us like sandpaper, and when we are in a raw or painful condition, one of God's most merciful acts is sending His help through people. "Of course," you say. "That's obvious. I mean, the people in the church I go to are my good friends, and I don't know what I would do without them. They are my core. They are so important in my life!"

Good for you. Now, hear the truth. Many people in your church come every Sunday and smile and talk with you, shake your hand, and even joke with you, but they are not having the same experience you just described. Every Sunday, they walk away feeling like they are just not good enough to deserve your attention. They see themselves as outside your group without a ticket to get in. They look okay and sound okay. But they are not okay. They believe they did not pass the test of being worthy of your friendship and your fellowship. Satan agrees with them, and he shows them lots of evidence that you don't have any interest in being friends with them, much less any time to devote to getting to know them. The devil told them that your friend list is full and that all the groups where relationships happen are also full. He also pointed out that you spoke to people in the rows in front of them and that you got close to them and then pretended they were not there.

Please do not get offended. I did not say you were a terrible, closed, and mean person, or that you did any of those things! I said people *perceive* themselves as not worthy of your friendship, and as being left out of all the relational mixes. Satan laughs... and quickly agrees with the thought he has planted to a calculated effect! Remember what we have learned about how people sometimes gather perceptual information? You are not trying to exclude. It is not your intention. But have you ever considered that Satan may distort things when we are not spiritually intentional?

The beast can prey on a sheep that is isolated, and the quickest way to isolate one of God's little lambs is to move him into a position where he *thinks* he is alone. I repeat. He *thinks* he is alone. And likely, his flock isn't thinking about it *at all*.

Satan has a strategy. Satan lies, distorts, brainwashes, deceives, and does not play by any rules. He engages in the dirtiest of warfare. A few pages back, I made the statement that sometimes Satan's army even includes good people who are momentarily detained and used before they know it. Looking at myself, I can most definitely see how I have sometimes unintentionally fallen into that snare.

I highly suspect many things that have happened in my life to hurt me were situations where another human being, without knowing it, fell into line with Satan's plan. When I view things that way, it helps me move past unforgiveness. However, even when people are successful at forgiving relational mistakes, Satan hopes to win on a diabolically different playing field. *He wants to use our experiences to shut down our mission.*

Battle Ready

The early church benefited from the unique attributes God placed in people. Peter was a guy who let God turn his tendencies toward impulsivity and assertiveness, along with his boisterous personality, into leadership qualities that sustained the early church. A brilliant orator, Paul's gifts included preaching, admonishing, and finding a platform in all kinds of situations. James modeled discipline, loyalty, and dependability. Other disciples displayed abilities in discernment and organization that contributed consequential functionality. Related to this book, of course, Barnabas had crucial qualities that we will explore more thoroughly in the discourse to come. God intentionally chose every one of those early church folks and anointed them with the power to accomplish something specific, essential, and important.

While today's Christians also have unique gifts for ordained missions, Satan is perhaps more aware of that fact than we are and more intent on stopping our work than we are on starting it. That said, spiritual reconnaissance is a pressing need for the church!

The term *reconnaissance* comes from a French word that means *recognize*. It is further defined as *observation of a region to locate an enemy or determine the strategic features of its position*. Spiritual reconnaissance, then, implies getting a fix on Satan. The church needs to learn where Satan is lurking and what he is trying to do. We must recognize the enemy is up to something heinous in our day and time, and we must determine what strategies he is using to work against God's plan.

I have often heard Christian people say that we don't need to worry about Satan because the Bible clearly states that he loses in the end. There are two tactical problems with that kind of thinking. First, we need to recognize that what we do and how we respond to God's call on our lives may have a direct impact on how long we will be required to endure the conflict in this earthly realm. Second, getting in line with God's plan certainly has the potential to propel God's mission and reduce human carnage.

Here are a few *landmines* that Satan can plant through what enters the human mind. It is vitally important to stay *alert* because Mr. Evil is an absolute expert in using such deceptive weaponry against God's mission and our intended purposes:

Isolation: a sense of being alone and without connection to others.

Perversion: a temptation to distort or ignore what the Bible says or accept contorted ideas to justify one's actions.

Lack of purpose: a perception that one does not matter and does not have any effect on the world around him.

No place to serve: the belief that others have filled all the places, and one is not needed.

Worthlessness: an idea that a person has nothing of value to offer.

Separation: the sense that one is not connected to others, or that there is a need to hide from others.

Segregation: the compulsion to restrict relationships to a specific comfort zone.

Loneliness: the sense that one is separated from others or that one is not known, wanted, or cared about.

Paralysis: the condition in which emotional pain or fear keeps one immobilized.

Atrophy: a failure to use one's gifts for a long time has created the deception of incapacity.

Trauma: an experience of intense pain has caused immobilization.

Self-centeredness: a focus on oneself that directs energy away from others and toward self-interests, pleasure, or attention-seeking.

Make no mistake. Satan is always at work looking for someone to devour, and he lurks dangerously in the territory between the ears. It is time for Christians to realize that they cannot leave awareness, defense, and strategic work to chance. We need to enable the weapons God gave us and make a firm commitment to serve. When we embrace our God-given purposes and help others to do so, God's mission goes forward in power.

Chapter 14

Leaning into Barnabas Perspectives

Now, do you ever wish, like I do, that you could somehow transport yourself back to certain stories chronicled in the Bible and just be an observant fly on the wall? Sometimes, Bible writers just do not give me all the juicy details that I would like to know. For me, Acts 15:36-40 would have been a situation like that. Since limited information appears in the scriptural account, maybe you and I can just stretch our curious side a bit and imagine how this argument between Barnabas and Paul went down. Then let's conjure up how the conversation between Barnabas and John Mark might have unfolded after they left the good apostle Paul.

Apparently, during an earlier missionary journey with Barnabas and John Mark, Paul was *not impressed* when John Mark bailed on them at Perga. We do not know why John Mark took off and went back to Jerusalem because, again, the writer of Acts just did not give us enough detail. Perhaps John Mark got a little freaked out when Paul was trading punches with a sorcerer. Or maybe he got worried about his mother, or possibly he just did not feel like he was adding much to the venture.

At any rate, Paul was *not pleased!* He did not see John Mark as apostle material at that point. When Barnabas proposed that John Mark accompany Paul and himself on the second journey, I can just imagine the conversation that ensued. I'm sure Paul would have said something like, "You've got to be kidding me! Did we not just learn how immature this guy is? Did he not jump ship in the middle of our mission? I just don't see the spirit of the Lord in this guy, and we certainly don't need distractions from this work. You may be a little blind in this because John Mark is your relative."

I'm also sure that Barnabas would have countered with something like, "I understand the way you feel, brother, but are we not all being shaped and formed for this work? John Mark is still just a big kid, and I don't think any of the rest of us can brag about perfection, either. John Mark has promise that God wants to use."

I wonder if Paul might have had a touch of selfishness way down deep. I can fully imagine that having a friend who was constantly focused on fanning your flame would be a tremendous comfort during challenging missionary journeys like those assigned to Barnabas and Paul. Paul probably did not even recognize it in himself, but it is certainly possible that he did not especially want to share that kind of personal fuel with a cousin that Barnabas loved and invested in.

At any rate, the disagreement between Paul and Barnabas remained non-negotiable. Paul chose a new mission companion in Silas, while Barnabas took his cousin John Mark and launched toward Cyprus.

I would also like to have heard the conversations on the journey with Barnabas and John Mark! I imagine John Mark might have thrown out words like, "Wow, I really blew it with the big guy, didn't I?" And I expect Barnabas would have said, "Paul only has eyes to press on with what he understands to be important. He is giving his all, but he sometimes just does not realize that others are not shaped like him. Besides, don't you see? Now God has just doubled his blessings! Now He has *two important* missions going on and we get to be a part of that! Don't worry about Paul. God totally has his ear, and God will always tell him to do what is right."

Maybe John Mark wondered, "But what if he is right about me? What if I *am* weak and immature? What if I don't have what it takes?" I am sure Barnabas would have said something like, "Look, John Mark, you locked in on Jesus years ago, long before Paul understood his truth. You saw Jesus at work. You saw him heal. His disciples have been all around you for years, and you saw the soldiers carry him out of Gethsemane to his death. You know all about his resurrection, and I believe with all my heart that the Holy Spirit has been working in you for a long time to get you ready for the work you are going to do. I one hundred percent believe in you, cousin, and we are going to walk together and work together on whatever journey God has for us. We should just pray that Paul is blessed in his efforts, and we are blessed in ours. God is going to do something amazing with you, and I cannot wait to see what He has in mind! My cousin is going to be a mighty man of God! Your job, John Mark, is just to obey and let God work out the rest before you."

Now, I don't know about *you*, but I need a cousin like *that!* That's an example of person-to-person fuel that causes *potential* to explode into *productivity!* Every single human being needs a miner of his worth. Everybody needs an encourager and a person to dust him off when he has made mistakes. Everyone needs a person to vouch for him and walk beside him. And each one of us needs someone to have *faith* in him and faith that God will bring forth the *best* in him. Everyone needs a *Barnabas*.

Friends, God is the *Creator*. He created all that exists, and He created each of us in His image. The thought that God channels His creativity into us and that we get to be a small part of God's intricate plan is incredibly exciting to me. The knowledge that the Holy Spirit comes to us, activates something in us, and brings forth skills that can be used in kingdom work is both humbling and daunting. In this knowledge are issues that we, as Christians, should see as our pliable challenge. First, and most obviously, we are to increase the numbers of people in this world who, by profession of faith, *invite* the Holy Spirit to inhabit their lives and to bring forth talents, gifts, and energies. Second, it is critical to help people with the practical components of *using* what the Holy Spirit activates. As a Christian community, we need to find more ways to be strategic about

- helping people *discover* their gifts
- helping people *connect* their gifts to God's mission
- supporting people in *developing* their gifts to new levels and for new *purposes*
- becoming spiritual *catalysts* for activating what God has placed in his people for *His* purposes
- removing obstacles and *opposing the spirits* that inhibit people from seeing their gifts and using them

Now consider the words that describe the master of spiritual partnership:

"Barnabas was a good man, full of the Holy Spirit…"

We have, in Barnabas, an example of a human vessel into whom God poured His Holy Spirit for the mission of mining gifts in others. Mining, as we know it, is not a very glamorous job. It is often dirty work. Mining involves close contact with dirt and mud to get to a precious substance. But when gold, silver, jewels, and other precious commodities are revealed, most do not continue to focus on the dirty part of the process. This is also true with the Barnabas Effect.

We often admire remarkable people and their accomplishments that benefit humanity, but we do not always get around to recognizing that either the Holy Spirit breathed something into being or that there was someone who saw a flicker of what the Holy Spirit placed in a person and fanned it into flame. We somehow miss the mud wrestling that came before the breakthrough.

The mining process is all over the Bible. Thanks to Satan, God did not have a single perfect human being to use in the development of His grand plan. No, there was not even *one!* So, when we see moments in the Bible when God chose unlikely human partners, consider that *any* human partner was unlikely. Fortunately, the creative power of the Holy Spirit, according to the will of the Father, can use *any* substance to bring *anything* into being according to its God-given purpose. That includes frail, dirty, disgusting human beings with all kinds of flaws. If the Son of God could use dirt and spit to open a man's eyes, can he not, through His love, use a human made from dirt for any purpose He desires?

Could it be that the Barnabas element that was so essential in the early church needs to be revived so that the organism called the church can produce more vibrant health and effectiveness? Does the church not exist in a social environment that is at least as hostile today as it was when it first began? How, then, do we put the *Barnabas* back in the church so that it is better equipped to withstand and vaporize Satan in his quest to destroy its resources?

How can this element help to ensure that the church fulfills its purpose?

As we have discussed, people need to be *seen* by others and have someone *mining* for the best in them, even if the miners need to go through dirt or rocks to get to the gold. People need to experience the power of *investment* in them by others. And further, they need careful escort to their God-given purposes by people full of the Holy Spirit. According to scripture, Barnabas was a desired mission companion because his nature was to provide all these things to people around him, and today's church could most definitely benefit from calling forth a Barnabas vigor in its work. We will now examine *elements* that bring forth the power of human resources. We move forward to find the character of Barnabas in people within our churches so that we can increase and propel God's mission even in the middle of unprecedented opposition from Satan.

As we just mentioned, scripture purposefully paints Barnabas in contrast to other characters from the first time we meet him. While others selfishly held something back, Barnabas gave all he had. The commitment he made to follow Christ was total and pure. In the book of Acts, he shines as one who gave himself totally to the cause of Christ with no other agenda but to serve the Savior. He was full of the Holy Spirit, and he gave the Holy Spirit complete permission to guide, teach, and use him. Let me repeat that key issue. Barnabas had no other intention but to serve the Savior by allowing the Holy Spirit to guide him and use him. Barnabas understood that the commission of the early church was singular according to words that came directly from Christ. It was to *make disciples* of all nations by preaching the good news about Jesus and by walking in the light delivered to the world by Christ. Barnabas took that seriously and did his work with simplicity. He met people one-on-one and allowed the Holy Spirit in him to minister individually and personally to those he encountered. It was as if every time Barnabas met a person, he asked the Holy Spirit,

> "What would you have me do for him?"

> "How would you have me feed this sheep?"

Chapter 15

Feed These Sheep

As we think of *feeding people*, we next recall the stories about Jesus feeding the multitudes. This story appears in all four gospels. That is helpful for us because, when any event happens, we know that each witness remembers the event a little differently based on his own perceptions. We benefit from that tendency in this case because there are more details we can discover through each of the different accounts.

Here are all the gospel versions for convenient comparison:

MATTHEW'S VERSION

As soon as Jesus heard the news, he left in a boat to a remote area to be alone. But the crowds heard where he was headed and followed on foot from many towns. Jesus saw the huge crowd as he stepped from the boat, and he had compassion on them and healed their sick.

That evening the disciples came to him and said, "This is a remote place, and it's already getting late. Send the crowds away so they can go to the villages and buy food for themselves."

But Jesus said, "That isn't necessary—you feed them."

"But we have only five loaves of bread and two fish!" they answered.

"Bring them here," he said. Then he told the people to sit down on the grass. Jesus took the five loaves and two fish, looked up toward heaven, and blessed them. Then, breaking the loaves into pieces, he gave the bread to the disciples, who distributed it to the people. They all ate as much as they wanted, and afterward, the disciples picked up twelve baskets of leftovers. About 5,000 men were fed that day, in addition to all the women and children!

(Matthew 14:13-21 NLV)

MARK'S VERSION

The apostles returned to Jesus from their ministry tour and told him all they had done and taught. Then Jesus said, "Let's go off by ourselves to a quiet place and rest awhile." He said this because there were so many people coming and going that Jesus and his apostles didn't even have time to eat.

So they left by boat for a quiet place, where they could be alone. But many people recognized them and saw them leaving, and people from many towns ran ahead along the shore and got there ahead of them. Jesus saw the huge crowd as he stepped from the boat, and he had compassion on them because they were like sheep without a shepherd. So he began teaching them many things.

Late in the afternoon his disciples came to him and said, "This is a remote place, and it's already getting late. Send the crowds away so they can go to the nearby farms and villages and buy something to eat."

But Jesus said, "You feed them."

"With what?" they asked. "We'd have to work for months to earn enough money to buy food for all these people!"

"How much bread do you have?" he asked. "Go and find out."

They came back and reported, "We have five loaves of bread and two fish."

Then Jesus told the disciples to have the people sit down in groups on the green grass. So they sat down in groups of fifty or a hundred.

Jesus took the five loaves and two fish, looked up toward heaven, and blessed them. Then, breaking the loaves into pieces, he kept giving the bread to the disciples so they could distribute it to the people. He also divided the fish for everyone to share. They all ate as much as they wanted, and afterward, the disciples picked up twelve baskets of leftover bread and fish. A total of 5,000 men and their families were fed.

(Mark 6:30-39 NLV)

LUKE'S VERSION

When the apostles returned, they told Jesus everything they had done. Then he slipped quietly away with them toward the town of Bethsaida. But the crowds found out where he was going, and they followed him. He welcomed them and taught them about the Kingdom of God, and he healed those who were sick.

Late in the afternoon the twelve disciples came to him and said, "Send the crowds away to the nearby villages and farms, so they can find food and lodging for the night. There is nothing to eat here in this remote place."

But Jesus said, "You feed them."

"But we have only five loaves of bread and two fish," they answered. "Or are you expecting us to go and buy enough food for this whole crowd?" For there were about 5,000 men there.

Jesus replied, "Tell them to sit down in groups of about fifty each." So the people all sat down. Jesus took the five loaves and two fish, looked up toward heaven, and blessed them. Then, breaking the loaves into pieces, he kept giving the bread and fish to the disciples so they could distribute it to the people. They all ate as much as they wanted, and afterward, the disciples picked up twelve baskets of leftovers!

(Luke 9:12-17 NLV)

JOHN'S VERSION

After this, Jesus crossed over to the far side of the Sea of Galilee, also known as the Sea of Tiberias. A huge crowd kept following him wherever he went, because they saw his miraculous signs as he healed the sick. Then Jesus climbed a hill and sat down with his disciples around him. (It was nearly time for the Jewish Passover celebration.) Jesus soon saw a huge crowd of people coming to look for him. Turning to Philip, he asked, "Where can we buy bread to feed all these people?" He was testing Philip, for he already knew what he was going to do.

Philip replied, "Even if we worked for months, we wouldn't have enough money to feed them!"

Then Andrew, Simon Peter's brother, spoke up. "There's a young boy here with five barley loaves and two fish. But what good is that with this huge crowd?"

"Tell everyone to sit down," Jesus said. So they all sat down on the grassy slopes. (The men alone numbered about 5,000.) Then Jesus took the loaves, gave thanks to God, and distributed them to the people. Afterward he did the same with the fish. And they all ate as much as they wanted. After everyone was full, Jesus told his disciples, "Now gather the leftovers, so that nothing is wasted." So they picked up the pieces and filled twelve baskets with scraps left by the people who had eaten from the five barley loaves.

> *When the people saw him do this miraculous sign, they exclaimed, "Surely, he is the Prophet we have been expecting!"*
>
> (John 6:1-14 NLV)

Can we consider a meaningful connection that struck me as I was reading this story? We know that Jesus saw a multitude of people, had compassion on them and engaged with them to teach and heal. But when the disciples thought it was time to send the crowd away so they could get something to eat, three of the gospel accounts record that Jesus said to His disciples: "You feed them."

In two gospels, it says that a disciple (Phillip) responded with a statement that almost sounded like, "Are you kidding? It would take more than half a year's wages to buy enough bread for each one to have a bite!" (Mark 6:37 and John 6:7) That was the general reaction of the Lord's twelve protégés. However, it sounds like in all four accounts, the disciples are also responding to a question that must have been something like "What do we have among us?"

> "But we have only five loaves of bread and two fish!" they answered. (Matthew)
>
> "We have five loaves of bread and two fish."(Mark)
>
> "But we have only five loaves of bread and two fish," they answered. (Luke)
>
> "There's a young boy here with five barley loaves and two fish. But what good is that with this huge crowd?" (John)

Scripture confirms these details:

1. Jesus had compassion for the crowd. In the gospel of Mark, it even says that Jesus had compassion on them because they were like sheep without a shepherd.

2. Jesus told the disciples "*You* feed them."

3. The disciples were responding to a question from Jesus that must have been something like, "What do we have among us?"

And the fourth fact? Well, specifically stated in Matthew and implied in all the other versions, there is a command from Jesus delivered *after* the "What do we have?" question. Matthew 14:18 records that Jesus said:

"Bring them here to me."

Let's remember that at this time in Jesus' ministry, he has just started training his disciples. He has sent them out once with specific instructions. They have now returned to Him for a little rest from their first efforts and for their next phase of training. On top of everything else, Jesus knows that John the Baptist is dead and that prophecies are being fulfilled at a rapid pace.

From the perspective of a teacher, the story of feeding the multitudes appears to capitalize on what educators call a teachable moment. Jesus wants His students to dig deep and figure something out. Three of the accounts (Matthew, Mark, and Luke) record that the disciples told Jesus the crowd needed to be sent away so they could go into towns and villages and find food. Again, these three accounts record that Jesus responds, "You feed them."

One of the gospel writers remembers the experience a little differently and says Jesus asked, "Where can we *buy* bread?" to feed these people. As a teacher, I can't help but wonder if that was exactly what Jesus said. I can't help but question if it was Jesus who used the word *buy*, because teachers rarely mention a solution when posing this kind of question. Based on the other disciples' recollection of the situation, I wonder if it is more likely that Jesus may have said something like, "So, how shall we *feed* all these people?" I wonder if the question "Where can we *buy*?" possibly came from a disciple based on his own usual experiences and thought processes. (Example: Ask a child how to get French fries, and an experience-laden response might be "*buy* some at McDonalds.") Or perhaps Jesus posed the question exactly that way. Maybe he wanted to emphasize that their resources were emphatically inadequate for the need.

In my imagination, I *see* all those people and some tired disciples with a very immature understanding. I *hear* a conversation that might have sounded like this:

> *Disciples: "Master, it is getting late. We should send these people away. They are going to need to eat."*
>
> *Jesus: "You are right, my friends. So, how could we feed them?"*
>
> *Disciples: "Where in the world could we buy enough food for this crowd? And how could we buy it?"*
>
> *Jesus: My question, friends, was, "How can we feed them?" And now listen to what I am saying. You feed them.*
>
> *Disciples: With what can we feed a crowd like this?*
>
> *Jesus: What do you have?*

> *(After researching this in their environment, Andrew finds a boy with a small amount of food.)*
>
> *Andrew: "It looks like all we have is five loaves and two fish that a little boy brought with him."*
>
> *Jesus: "Bring what you have to me."*

In this story, I believe Jesus was teaching the disciples something important about what to do to begin his church when he left this earth. He was saying here what he would say a little differently in John 21. He was saying, *"Feed my sheep."* The disciples were still thinking with carnal minds and little understanding about what their role was about to be. Jesus, however, was trying to teach them how they would spread the good news of salvation to the world. He was telling them they were to bring him whatever they had, including their gifts, their talents, their personalities, their tenacity, their enthusiasm, their love for Him, their weaknesses, and their strengths. They were to bring what they had (even though they had limitations), put what they had into *His* hands, and watch what He could do with it.

> *You feed them.*
>
> *Do not worry.*
>
> *Bring me what you have, and*
>
> *Watch what I can do with it.*

This lesson must have been quite important in the overall disciple training program because Jesus taught it twice, with subtle and significant differences. John 6:25-41 indicates that Jesus also gave his students another lesson and directly told them what was going to be on the test. He said he was the Bread of Life sent to the entire human world through the love of Father God. Further, He explained that, unlike the bread provided in the time of Moses (manna), His miracles were not about filling bellies at all. He was the Bread of Life. He was also the route to abundant life on earth and in eternity. It looks like Jesus even did an end-of-unit review of these lessons in Matthew 16:8-10:

> *"Aware of their discussion, Jesus asked, 'You of little faith, why are you talking among yourselves about having no bread? Do you still not understand? Don't you remember the five loaves for the five thousand, and how many basketfuls you gathered? Or the seven loaves for the four thousand, and how many basketfuls you gathered? How is it you don't understand that I was not talking to you about bread?'"*

(Matthew 16:8-10 NIV)

Because there are two stories recounted in the gospels about feeding multitudes, scholars have proposed an enlightening interpretation of the different numbers used in the stories. The feeding of the five thousand started with five loaves of bread to represent the five books of the Law. The twelve remaining baskets represent the twelve tribes of Israel and the twelve chosen disciples, all Jews, who experienced the revelation of the new covenant in Jesus. In the feeding of the four thousand, the seven loaves denote the perfection of God's love through Jesus' sacrifice for our sins. The leftovers filled seven baskets, signifying the proliferation of God's love and acceptance to all people who would receive Jesus as the Messiah. Interestingly, the accounts of these two stories use different words for the baskets in each miracle. In the story about the five thousand, the Greek word *kophinos*, which means small baskets, identifies the baskets for the leftovers. In the story of the four thousand, however, the seven baskets for leftovers are the Greek word *spuris*, meaning a large, flexible basket. Salvation was offered to all people, along with the invitation to join the mission. Everything in the Word is alive with purpose!

Looking even closer, Jesus, the ultimate teacher, was laying a foundation. He was putting concepts in place to help *all* believers understand they are joint heirs in a **new covenant.** Believers in Christ not **only** *inherit God's mission and the leadership roles* for it (*bechora*), but also all *the resources* (*berachot*) needed to fulfill it. He said that those who believe in him and place themselves in his hands (even with all their inadequacies) will have all the resources needed to complete the mission of feeding the sheep. Jesus is subtly telling His disciples to not only *feed the sheep* but to help the sheep *feed other sheep*.

Bottom line? Jesus was teaching His disciples, starting with the twelve men in the story and expanding to all disciples who would later read these stories, that there is a world out there filled with people who need to be fed. They need to be fed with the *Bread of Life*. Jesus says to each of us:

> *You do it.*
>
> *Bring me what you have,*
>
> *Put it in my hands, and*
>
> *Watch what I can do with it.*

Before we leave this story, I have to stop and be thankful for two subtle messages recorded in John's gospel. John 6:12

records these words of Jesus, and I am convinced he was not just talking about bread.

"...Let nothing be wasted."

Again, I am sure he was not just talking about bread.

To that point, at the gospel moment when Jesus fed the multitudes, we have not officially met our hero, Barnabas. However, I propose that you have already encountered his very nature in someone else. Remember Andrew? What does John's account tell us about him? He saw a boy who had something. He brought that something to Jesus. Even though he had questions, he did not toss aside what the boy had. He just brought it to Jesus... and he put what the boy had in a position to be used by God.

Welcome to Barnabas Class 101!

Chapter 16

Barnabas 101

Dear Church.
You do it.
Figure out what you have.
Put it in my hands, and
watch what I can do with it.
Love,
Jesus

We have pounded the point that Satan often attacks God's people. They get "clocked," knocked down, and laid out. I would wager anyone reading this book right now has been there many times. People can find their mission for God at least temporarily stalled out, damaged, or neutralized. They can feel abandoned, isolated, imprisoned, or they can become profoundly *discouraged*. There are likely people around you right now who have great passion, exciting potential, and creative ideas for something that could be turned into purposeful work for the Lord. But so many won't speak it, dream it, or do it because they are locked in a prison of *doubt* about what God has placed in them.

Yes. That is where people can be. But is there an antidote to these situations? Suppose something shifted. What if someone allowed himself to be used by God to rescue another from a place of discouragement and paralysis? Consider the impact if one of God's people made one gesture that pulled someone out of an immobilized state with an act of simple, strategic encouragement. What if the hurting person could meet a *Barnabas*?

Better still, what if Christians could learn to value and *pursue* spiritual search and rescue for *others*? Believe me, friends, there are *others*. There are tons of them. Sadly, both you and I will likely be in a position this week where we will either need rescue or could rescue someone else. Unfortunately, here is the rest of the story:

Satan *wants* people to be stalled out and resigned to failure and worthlessness. He *wants* God's people to feel impotent, paralyzed, and without purpose. He does *not* want people to be free for joyful obedience to God's *purpose* for them. And don't put it past Satan to conscript good folks like you and me to *cause* the immobilization of others in their mission walk.

There are thousands of God's army troops who stand neutralized, frozen, and incapacitated for the purposes God has assigned them. They may not know their purpose or how to connect their talents, gifts, and energies to God's plan for them. They may not even be aware that they have something inside them that God placed there to bring him glory. Perhaps you remember the metaphor introduced in chapter one. It was about people being "frozen" in the game of tag, where they could no longer be useful to one team in the game. More exactly, they could no longer be active and useful in the game until one of their team members saw their condition, touched them, and freed them for valuable actions in the game. That's a great picture of what Barnabas folks can do to mobilize God's *people* for God's *mission*.

Barnabas people learn to peruse the world for those who might be *tagged out*. They invite the spirit to lead them to people and show them how to interact with people so they can help them discover their kingdom gifts. They *stop and render aid* so that one of God's servants can become activated (or perhaps resuscitated) for his role in God's mission.

BECOMING A BARNABAS PERSON:

Maybe you are wondering how someone can become a Barnabas person. The next chapters will address exactly that. We will explore behaviors that both help and hinder others in the discovery and application of their God-given gifts and purposes.

I will state that I *Barnabas* naturally around kids. They draw that nature out of me. I love to *mine* when I am with younger folks, but

I also confess it does not come as easily to me with adults. Around adults, I can be more like a *Peter*. I can be impulsive, quick to open my mouth, and quick to *draw the sword*. I can be even *quicker* to draw swift and humiliating discipline. More often, I am afraid of the *Peter* side of me, and I choose to sit in the corner, terrified of the big, bad adults around me. That is a good reason to learn all I can about ways to create Barnabas behavior in my life! So, I am trying to step out of awkwardness and learn to take on Barnabas roles that flow from me naturally. I propose that even those of us who may not think we are natural Barnabas types can certainly harness our traits and train them for useful Barnabas work.

Perhaps you are thinking about your traits and wondering if you can be a Barnabas person. The answer is an emphatic and resounding *yes*. Being a Barnabas person can be learned and churned. There are many things you can learn to be intentional about, and when we ask God to fill us with His Holy Spirit and give us opportunities to use our natural gifts, Barnabas things seem to happen.

Think about the Processes

Our next pursuit will be to describe the positive, intentional components we can build into Barnabas work in the kingdom. To begin, we should define the Barnabas Effect. It is

> "...an effect realized when a person has experiences that ignite or revive potential and connect him to purpose. It is achieved through processes like intentional mining, resuscitation, advocacy, investment, facilitation, and encouragement."

We will continue by defining and breaking down the processes listed in this definition. Then, in the next chapter, we will unpack each Barnabas behavior for practical use.

INTENTIONAL MINING AND RESUSCITATION

Intentional mining has to do with discovery, and discovery requires awareness, detection, digging in beyond the surface, moving extraneous things out of the way, and separating something of value from the other things around it. It might involve helping a person *see* his potential, and it might mean reviving a person who has somehow become separated from his kingdom purpose.

ADVOCACY

This is the process of promotion. It requires both presenting something and showcasing its value. It may require the provision of evidence, and it may require creating a vision of potential.

INVESTMENT

Investment requires pouring resources into people and waiting patiently for results. These resources might include time, training, confidence building, mentorship, tangible assets, and strategic encouragement.

FACILITATION

Facilitation is working with parts to make them work better together. It involves communication and connecting people to resources like training, mentorship, organizations, or essential expertise. Facilitation helps purpose flow into action more easily.

ENCOURAGEMENT

Encouragement provides the fuel that motivates a person to *use* his potential. It can include communication, inspiration, companionship, partnership, and any of the other processes described above.

Barnabas people are not necessarily just people with kind words, an empathetic nature, and loving arms! They can be people who push others toward action, challenge others, and create plans to make something happen. Barnabas people can persuade, negotiate, and navigate steps toward getting something done. They can train someone or provide resources. They could even be people who know how to define process steps, connect diverse entities, enlist organizations, access funding, and coordinate process procedures. Barnabas people can also provide inspiration, motivation, and nourishment in all different forms. Don't even think Barnabas people are just soft, *touchy-feely* people. Barnabas work is *bold* kingdom work. As we explore each behavioral manifestation of the Barnabas Effect, the challenge should be to consider how we can each use our natural gifts to contribute to the enterprise. Now, please forgive me for beginning our in-depth discussion of the topic in the negative. I ask for a bit of grace as I mention a few things that can *inhibit* the Barnabas Enterprise in a big way and keep us from the work we *could* be accomplishing.

First, Do No Harm

The phrase "First, Do No Harm" has traditionally been associated with professional ethics for physicians. In summary of the concept, it is the standard for how a physician should approach treatment. It says that a competent physician must always:

- consider if a treatment might produce any foreseeable harm

- determine the highest standard of care based on the most current knowledge about both the individual and the treatment

- remain aware of *knowledge gaps,* or what is unknown about the issue

Wouldn't it be great if people could adhere to a standard like that in interaction with other people?

Remember: Satan conscripts his army, and he often detains God's troops (you and me) just long enough to do strategic dirty work. I suspect that one of his favorite ways to do this is by causing the human mouth to go astray.

God can close the mouths of lions. Unfortunately, Satan can often *open* the mouths of *Christians* at just the right time and in just the wrong way, resulting in human damage in the home camp. And, if you remember our previous discussion, he also uses the personal pain of the hearer to distort messages, so they cause even more inflammation of the mind. This phenomenon is like an atomic bomb. First, there is a damaging impact, followed by the destruction of radioactive effects.

Do No Harm.

> *"Do not use harmful words, but only helpful words, the kind that build up and provide what is needed, so that what you say will do good to those who hear you. And do not make God's Holy Spirit sad; for the Spirit is God's mark of ownership on you, a guarantee that the Day will come when God will set you free."*
>
> (Ephesians 4:29-30 Good News Translation)

Scripture says God wants us to use the mouth to build people up, grow their faith, grow their courage, and empower their boldness to serve. Did you note the words in the verse above about making God's Holy Spirit sad? I am very sure that when our words end up giving Satan any moment of victory, we grieve God's heart.

I am also certain that misguided words from well-intentioned believers have often caused people to choose the spectator seats in the church. If Christian people want to become *Barnabas* folks, it would be a promising idea to do what the doctors took an oath to do. It would be highly impactful to never let words pass through our lips without *carefully* weighing any foreseeable harm!

Barnabas folks should go beyond that to determine if their words meet the "highest standard of care" that is described when the scripture says to use words that:

- provide help
- build up
- meet the needs of the hearer
- do good

It makes the Holy Spirit sad when we act in ways that hurt the body of Christ or cause any part to lose its function. Wouldn't it be great if folks could *"remain aware of knowledge gaps"* when they are interacting with others? I maintain it is quite common for people to sling comments, give opinions, and make judgments without knowing much about the people they are talking to or the people who are within earshot. Maybe a person was about to volunteer, and someone's words prompted a decision not to do so. A person may have wanted to contribute, and someone's words minimized what they could offer. Maybe words came out without understanding a person's pain or experience. Perhaps a church member thought he was being funny, clever, or wise and did not know the pain he was flinging unknowingly. So here is the question:

If we took the time to get to know each other better, bear each other's burdens, and share each other's pain, could we gain the trust of our fellow travelers and engage their potential more effectively?

Stop the Busy Signal

There was a recent Geico insurance commercial about two cowboys who were challenging each other to a gunfight. The problem in the scenario was that neither of them could work it into his calendar. The dialogue goes like this:

First cowboy: You and Me Partner. We meet center of town… high noon.

Second Cowboy: Hold on… Nope! Daisy's got lassoin' lessons at noon.

First cowboy: Ok. High two o'clock?

Second Cowboy: I got a spur fittin' at two o'clock. How's about three?

First Cowboy: I'm getting thrown through a saloon window at three.

(Commercial message: "We don't need any more overscheduling, but we all need more ways to save on insurance.")

Second cowboy: I can squeeze you in between swim class and Kevin's harp recital at three thirty.

Bystander: Thought we's eatin beans at three thirty?

2nd Cowboy: Right

1st cowboy: Tell you what. What about Tuesday?

If you want to see the entire commercial, go to: https://www.youtube.com/watch?v=E7twTm7f46k

Ok, that's funny in a commercial. It's funny because it's only a slight exaggeration of the truth! Have you tried to make friends with folks at church lately?

My commercial message:

We don't need any more scheduling, but everyone could use a lot more genuine connection.

I'm not slamming church folks. I *am* one! Unfortunately, Satan has a way of using unsuspecting people (like me and you) to carry out his purposes. What if that person who wanted to go to lunch with me wanted to talk about giving his life to Jesus? What if that human being was about to give up on himself or desperately needed to talk to someone about a crisis? Is there a possibility that the person who looked okay on the outside was about three steps from becoming suicidal? Ponder if that person was sitting on a gold mine of potential, a great idea, or incredible gifts God wanted him to use. What if you or I miss the opportunity to extend the love of Jesus and inadvertently aid in Satan's scheme to destroy something of value to God?

What if we are just too busy to be used by God for his purposes?

No Glory Grabbing

Of all the words in this book, I am most nervous about the ones I am about to write. On that note, I ask readers to forgive me in advance and extend grace because, as hard as I have tried to leave this out, something keeps pushing me to express what I am about to put right here on paper in front of God and everybody. I will say it as gently as I can. Pretty much everyone in the universe has experienced, in some place or some situation, the fear of being in the middle of the old playground ordeal called *last chosen*. You know what I mean. It is horrible to know you are standing on the playground when the most powerful, most connected, and most feared people are selecting their teams. These people are automatically chosen, never left out, and they choose others who are most likely to hold them in high regard because that supports the feeling of power they want. Woe to the kid in the situation who seems small, weak, or useless. Woe, also, to the kid who might be unknown or new. Woe to the kid who doesn't look or sound right or lacks connection to the right people. Worse yet, *woe* to the kid who might present some kind of opposition, however subtle, to the power position of the team chooser. And finally, WHOA to the kid who might not run fast or bat well but could analyze player tendencies and figure out how the team could work more effectively!

People have experienced this kind of scenario at school, work, in the community, in their families, and so forth. Folks come into churches with this experience hovering in their emotional background. They also sometimes find themselves in churches where, even if undiscovered, this phenomenon exists. People don't go out for the team because they don't want to be the ones not chosen. They may not engage because they see an organization that does not welcome their gifts. They may even sense they are not welcome because they present a threat to those who have found secure positions or those who want to control the way things are done.

There, I said it.

Sadly, I have experienced it, and, more sadly, I have also been guilty of it. Guess what? We don't own the ant farm, and neither do we own the dirt or any tunnel in it.

So, let's just quickly say:

Make room for all God's ants and the work they can do.

Could churches think about the avenues they employ to involve people? What are the church's tendencies in filling ministry opportunities and service positions? Is there an effort to help each member find a place to serve and a way to contribute?

If the same people show up over and over in all the areas of service, might it be prudent for the church to ask *why*? Is it that people are refusing to engage, or is it that some people always get there *first*? Is there a phantom idea hanging around that doing multiple jobs in the church is stacking up more rewards in heaven, so people should grab all they can? Or maybe we should ask another question. Do we limit the ministry possibilities in churches by trying to stuff people into a finite number of specific, pre-defined pigeonholes instead of creating pathways for all kinds of kingdom work?

I hope we will be moved to ponder that last thought *and* this next one. Jesus did not post an advertisement to enlist disciples. He did not go to the synagogue and ask for help to find the *right people*. Jesus *noticed* people around him and observed them both perceptually and *spiritually*. He interacted with them to discover hearts tunable to God and pliable for shaping. He invited people to engage, and he delighted in all the gifts God had lovingly placed in them.

We are here today because the least likely were invited to serve in the *unique* ways they were made. Jesus asked his followers to do things that suited the gifts *within* them while he sent *all* of them into kingdom work. Did Matthew use his gift of documenting and writing? Did Peter use his gifts of leadership, organization, passion, and tenacity? Can we give people the opportunity to pursue their kingdom purposes, too?

Whew! That discussion is behind us. Now, on to how we can individually create a positive *Barnabas Effect* in the lives of others.

Chapter 17

The Components of Barnabas Business I

The Barnabas Effect is an effect realized when a person has experiences that ignite or revive potential and connect him to purpose. It is achieved through processes like intentional mining, resuscitation, advocacy, investment, facilitation, and encouragement.

Barnabas Component 1: Mining and Resuscitation

A few years ago, my family bought a piece of property. About two seconds after we bought that property, we started asking ourselves what had momentarily caused us to be so deranged that we did! That property was ugly. Most of it was covered in a tangled mass of vegetation that rural folks call *shin'ry*. The place was so ugly that it barely even fit into *that* derogatory category. To be honest, we spent some months rather stymied by our stupidity before we even tried to improve the place.

One day, we somehow stopped focusing on the ugly. Instead, we noticed a group of trees in the middle of the ugly. We noticed they were big, shady, and quite attractive if you could block out the ugly around them, and we had a sudden urge to uncover them. At first, the process was painful (literally) because these trees were intensely entangled with thick, twisted, stickery briars. Remarkably, as we struggled to uncover trees, we discovered the briars could be cut from the bottom and pulled out of the trees with careful technique. Gradually, we progressed with our tool arsenal, from clippers to long loppers and then to battery-powered hedge trimmers. We found more suitable gloves and more armored clothing for the task. Then... the most crucial tool evolved: *motivation!*

We worked so hard that we just got lost in the work and the process became an intriguing challenge. Then, we looked up from our labors, and we were awestruck by pretty, green, shady *trees!* We had freed the trees, and they were beautiful.

In our part of the country, trees are gold. They are a scarce commodity, and the tree that gives cooling shade is a substantial luxury. Out of the *ugly*, something of value had emerged. Little by little, we continued to free the trees. Today, the property is no longer offensive! It is satisfying. It is satisfying, not just because it looks better, but because we uncovered beauty and usefulness that had been in prison for so long. We find it satisfying because every spring, the trees we uncovered burst forth with a green resurrection that shouts,

Thanks for rescuing us!

Thanks for resuscitating us for our purpose.

People can be just as entangled in ugly briars as our trees were. It is not the people who are ugly. It is the briars and thorns of life that have grown up to create a prison around them. Barnabas people put on their *people gloves* and use all the tools in their arsenal to free people from what has held them in captivity and away from their God-given purposes. They employ genuine interest, friendship, and attention to throw off what hinders so purpose can be revealed. What a beautiful mission to rescue people from the briars the world has used to entangle them and to free them to be beautiful, well-watered trees in the service of God.

> *"And he shall be like a tree planted by the rivers of water, that bringeth forth his fruit in his season; His leaf also shall not wither; And whatsoever he doeth shall prosper".*
>
> (Psalm 1:3)

Remember: Move the briars. Free the trees.

We have said that *intentional human mining* has to do with discovery. Discovery requires awareness, detection, and digging beyond the surface. It involves moving extraneous things out of the way and separating something of value from the other things around it that may hide it or keep it from being useful.

Mining has always been challenging work. If you are trying to get a mineral out of a mountain or a tree out of the briars, there is a physical challenge in that process. It may involve tools and machinery, and it usually requires *force* of some kind. When human mining takes place, there is also arduous work to be done, but the challenge is different because the process is relational, not physical. It requires *relationship*, not force.

In any mining process, the detection of a valuable substance is the first step. Subsequently, there are many hard tasks to bring something of value out of whatever is holding it hostage. Human mining requires a specialized detection process, and it does not come naturally to most people. It requires focusing on someone else. It might even involve the simple act of noticing them, followed by the intentional pursuit of a relationship. People in groups rarely focus on others. Most focus on what the speaker is saying and ask, "*What about me?*" People think about what affects *them*. They dwell on what they are going to *say*, or possibly what the group *thinks of them*. Humans are prone to *self-centered* thinking.

Mining in humans requires a shift. It requires hyper-focus on another person and intense observation. It also involves an intentional process that demands *question-driven thinking* about a person, followed by targeted conversation.

An example:

Pretend you are in a room where a focus group is discussing something, or you are on a committee that is trying to decide what needs to be done. What if you intently observed? What if you saw someone who made a significant difference in that committee, and you said something like this to him:

> *"I appreciated the way you brought out the different points of view in that meeting today. You listened so carefully to everyone and made sure you understood what their concerns were. The way you pursued every point of view and asked so many good questions inspired every single person in that meeting to respect other people and genuinely listen to find common ground. Few people could have negotiated that issue so well. I know that I saw things I had not seen before, and that made all the difference in the way I voted."*

When someone takes the time to notice another person's contribution and give him specific feedback about what he did well, two things happen. First, the person *thinks* about what he did. Second, he becomes more likely to repeat the behavior. He might even repeat it often enough to let it become a vocation or a calling in an arena where he is connected. The person might be better able to connect his ability to his God-given purpose or his kingdom work if someone added something like this to the feedback communication:

> *"That kind of ability to get people working together for solving problems could be so valuable in our church. We need to bring you in just to manage the communication."*

That is Barnabas work! Noticing abilities and then flashing them on a thought screen for a person to see creates possibility from potential.

Another example:

When I went into classrooms to teach guidance lessons, one of my very favorite things was observing kids in those groups. I loved to watch their reactions to the concrete illustrations I brought. I enjoyed watching their faces as I talked, and their reactions when I asked questions. Usually, I searched for a kid whose face and body language said he was bursting to respond, but whose demeanor told me he did not have the personal confidence to do so. I often wrote the student's name down. On another day, I would pull that same kid out of class to do two things. First, I would tell the student what I had noticed about him. I would mention what he had done that impressed me or what he did that helped me with the lesson. Second, I would tell the student about something at school where I believed he could contribute. Many times, I could connect kids to something that changed the way they *saw* themselves so they could *become* themselves. I found pleasure in those conversations, and in moving kids into a group with a specific enterprise or purpose. It always gave me immense joy to watch any kid move from an obscure existence to becoming a dynamic contributor.

I am convinced that this same process could be a step in discovering people who need to be connected to kingdom work. There are those of you who have a natural tendency toward this process, and you could implement it somewhere in your church relationships. These opportunities might be in obvious places, like Sunday school groups, life groups, or study groups. They might even occur through church-designed programs that promote them or in the flow of daily interaction, even outside the church.

Some of you might notice that you have a knack for paying attention to people as they interact in their small church groups. What if, instead of concentrating on what *you* will say next in groups, you asked questions of others to see what *they* had to say? Maybe you could discover what people could contribute and where that might lead them to serve.

Example 1: Seeing people and what they do well

Example questions:

- When you mentioned a minute ago that you "struggle" with that, what thoughts come to your mind that signal you are in a struggle?
- You said a minute ago that you really like _____. When have you done that before?

- You said your friend at work is quite important in your spiritual life. What does that friend do for you that makes a difference in your life?
- I'm curious. If I asked each one of you what you think God is asking you to do right now, how would you answer that?
- You mentioned a time when _____. How did you know that was important, and what did you decide to do?

There are no *magic* questions to ask people, but asking God what he wants you to find out about people might be a good place to start. You can find out what people do vocationally and what they like about their work. It is also revealing to find out when people have experienced the most euphoria in their lives. Interestingly, that can be a distinct marker that points directly to a God-given gift. If you work on a relationship with someone, you will usually notice something about them or *see something shiny* in them. You might even connect them to important kingdom work.

For those who want to get serious about human mining, using metacognitive questions like those described above will be a helpful skill. (Page 157, titled More Resources, offers more information about these powerful questions.) Using these powerful questions in groups and in personal conversations with people you want to *Barnabas* can reveal valuable information. Questions that help people think about their thinking are great tools to reveal strengths. And, as we have noted before, the Bible loudly says,

> "As a man thinketh in his heart, so is he."

Just remember that getting to what a person is thinking in his heart takes far more effort than getting to what might rattle from his head to his mouth. Remember: Move the briars. Free the trees.

A forward thought...

On one of my research rabbit trails, I found some interesting information about the California Gold Rush and I gleaned a few "nuggets" about mining. First, I learned that hundreds of people gave up or got killed before they ever got to the mining process in California. (I sure hope none of that happens to my readers!) I also learned that people who started mining by panning to scoop gold out of a stream often gave up quickly when the task changed to hard digging and busting through rock. Make no mistake. Mining can get hard! The other tidbit I picked up was that the Gold Rush started just after California became a state. How fortunate for California! Wouldn't it be great if mining for kingdom potential could start immediately after people have reached the state of salvation?

Barnabas Component 2: Advocacy

The words *recommend, support, back,* and *champion* will appear in the definition for *advocate. Champion* is an interesting word in the mix because it means to *fight or battle for another*. Barnabas did battle with key people to get Saul accepted into a group that would allow his purpose to emerge. He went beyond a standard recommendation. He went beyond letting Saul do the battle and just giving him support. Barnabas *championed* the unfolding purpose of Saul. Remember, advocacy is not just saying, "Great! Good luck with that!"

If I were going to look for an advocate, I might look for someone good at selling, marketing, creating webs of connection, or leveraging points of influence. These are people who can get something off the shelf, off the lot, out of the warehouse, and out of obscurity!

Let me give you a personal example. I have a friend that comes to mind when I think of this Barnabas role. He is always asking questions like, "What if you did this or that?" This guy reads voraciously to build all kinds of connections in his warehouse of thought. He is also a *bona fide promoter*. It comes naturally to him, and he does it with even simple things.

The friend I speak of likes the game of pickleball. As I understand it, pickleball is a rather recent interest for him, but he is absolutely *sold* on it. This gentleman learns all he can find out about this sport. He knows where all the courts are in our area, and he has many friends who play the game locally. This guy is aware of the schedules for all the places where pickleball happens every week in our city, and he has discovered the organizations and individuals that have pickleball courts. He can tell you about pickleball surfaces, pickleball equipment, pickleball shoes, and pickleball rules! He is all-out sold on pickleball and he wants others to be sold on it, too! If he knows your name, he is likely to pursue the subject of pickleball with you.

I barely knew this guy when he told me about pickleball and how I really should try it. He did not stop with just a casual mention, either. He worked hard to get me (a person he did not know all that well) to try this funny-sounding game. In conversations with other friends, I soon learned that this guy had been working on getting *them* to play pickleball, too! He gave us information about how we could try pickleball, and he continued to give very enthusiastic pitches to convince people (a lot of them) that they needed to try this game. I knew this guy was super serious about this pickleball thing when he invited me and my husband to come to a specific court so he could provide us with equipment, walk us through the game, and show us how to enjoy pickleball. He made still another interesting effort for the cause. When we finally showed up on a court to learn about pickleball, this guy had arranged for us to play with other pickleball *newbies* and, in our case, he had worked it out so that the people we were meeting were our best friends. That's a genius plan when people need a level of comfort to learn something new!

I am convinced that pickleball suppliers and the federation of the sport of pickleball need to meet my friend. I am also convinced that this friend won't give up on me until I have my feet firmly planted in the sport of pickleball. He is an incredible advocate for the game! Think about it. This person sees value in something, gathers information, promotes something, and connects people to both resources and other people for a desired outcome. Honestly, I cannot think of a better example of advocacy. It can be powerfully reframed for God's purposes.

Some people are just natural advocates. They may have many connections or diverse ways of connecting people to helpful entities. Effective advocates can connect people with similar interests and ideas, or they may have a link to funding. Some might even have skills for creating an organization essential for someone's mission. No matter what contributions the person might offer, I would know the person is a true Barnabas if he could perform advocacy with the enthusiasm of my pickleball friend.

There are those out there connected and respected in such a way to secure a seat for someone on the flight to purpose. There are those who know strategic people for making something happen. If they don't know them, they can find them. If it is not a person who could offer critical help, it might be an organization, an entity of expertise, or a small group of people who have either mighty faith or muscle connections. A person with resources can get someone plugged in.

You, Barnabas advocate, are a person who can give a human being and his God-given purpose the platform to launch!

Chapter 18

The Components of Barnabas Business II

The Barnabas Effect is an effect realized when a person has experiences that ignite or revive potential and connect him to purpose. It is achieved through processes like intentional mining, resuscitation, advocacy, investment, facilitation, and encouragement.

Barnabas Component 3: Investment

This part of the Barnabas process is likely the one that people resist the most. Quite possibly, the enemy uses one of his best strategies to get folks to resist engagement in this important part of Barnabas business. The name of that enemy strategy is *greed*. Unfortunately, what people *have*, they often want to keep. They want to keep what they *have* because their mindset is:

- What they *have* belongs to *them*.
- What they *have*, they have gained with their own efforts.
- What they *have* is limited and finite.
- What they *have* is diminished when they *give* it to someone else.

A Barnabas person, in contrast, has this mindset:

- What they *have* belongs to God, and they are privileged to steward it.
- What they *have* gained is through God's grace and provision.
- What they *have* is a portion of God's infinite, unlimited resources.
- What they *have* is multiplied and proliferated in God's hands, just like the loaves and the fish were in the feeding of the multitudes.

Upon the subtle direction of the enemy, people become greedy, selfish, and stingy with things like money, influence, energy, attention, and time. To the point of this section, *all* those things are needed for *investment*. Some of us may not have much money in our personal pockets, but God has deep, unlimited pockets for those who are full of faith. Moreover, few of us are without energy, attention, and time. It is not *lack* that keeps us from serving in this area. It is *choice*. We often choose not to direct what we have to kingdom work.

Truthfully, all the Barnabas components involve investment. Mining requires time and effort for building relationships. Advocacy requires labor to promote people and connect resources to missions. Facilitation requires focus and energy toward making things work more efficiently, and *encouragement* is an investment that motivates every effort. Barnabas was a remarkable example of investment! He was full of the Holy Spirit and always focused on giving what he had.

> *"(Barnabas) sold a field he owned and brought the money and put it at the apostles' feet."*
>
> (Acts 4:37)

To paraphrase and extend the meaning of that scripture, Barnabas gave up what he had (material wealth, energy, attention, and time) to give it to somebody else who had needs related to God's mission.

One Sunday morning, my Sunday school class was looking at the parable of the talents. Before I realized it, I had commented that this parable disturbed me more than anything in the Bible. Though I immediately wished my mouth were not so connected to every straying thought, a few people in the class offered what they could to help me with what they assumed was on my mind. I was thankful for their efforts. However, what was stirring in my mind was more than what was on the surface, and I knew my disturbance was connected to this book project. I mulled this scripture over for a long time. Look at what it says:

"For it will be like a man going on a journey, who called his servants and entrusted to them his property. To one he gave five talents, to another two, to another one, to each according to his ability. Then he went away. He who had received the five talents went at once and traded with them, and he made five talents more. So also he who had the two talents made two talents more. But he who had received the one talent went and dug in the ground and hid his master's money. Now after a long time the master of those servants came and settled accounts with them. And he who had received the five talents came forward, bringing five talents more, saying, 'Master, you delivered to me five talents; here, I have made five talents more.' His master said to him, 'Well done, good and faithful servant. You have been faithful over a little; I will set you over much. Enter into the joy of your master.' And he also who had the two talents came forward, saying, 'Master, you delivered to me two talents; here, I have made two talents more.' His master said to him, 'Well done, good and faithful servant. You have been faithful over a little; I will set you over much. Enter into the joy of your master.' He also who had received the one talent came forward, saying, 'Master, I knew you to be a hard man, reaping where you did not sow, and gathering where you scattered no seed, so I was afraid, and I went and hid your talent in the ground. Here, you have what is yours.'"

(Matthew 25:14-25 ESV)

Two things rattled around in my head as I read. First, the master *distributed* something to the servants that belonged to him. The master gave the servants something. The servants did not earn it. Recognize it or not, all we *are* and everything in our reach belongs to God. Second, the master gave *resources* to the servants, "each according to his ability." Ability is *a means or a skill* to do something. The master did not assign his property based on the means or skills of just anybody. Instead, he took into consideration what *means* one specific individual had and what *skills* that person had. He did not ask the person with one talent to use the means and skills of the guy with five talents. He asked him to *use* his *own* means and skills. Means is about *how*. It is a method or a *way* of doing something. It seems the master was not concerned about quantities in this story. He was concerned about *use!*

The other word that struck me in the parable was *trade*. (Note: The word *trade* also appears in the King James Version, the New King James Version, and the NASB version uses the words, "did business with.") Trade denotes that talents function as *currency*. Currency has value and can be exchanged for something else of value. Though money is the image people connect with the word currency, it is only a symbol of another value. The definition we should examine refers to a human currency that assigns value to things like interactions, relationships, and personal contributions. Instead of dollar bills, we are now working with things like time, energy, and social capital. We are bringing focus to connections, experiences, and *opportunities*. All these things are to be used and shared faithfully. It is the ultimate stewardship of what God breathes into our lives.

What if we looked at the parable from a slightly altered perspective? What if we thought about it as if it were about currency, means, and skill? Could it be that God gives us *currency* to *exchange?* We are to use our God-given skills and our *way*, or maybe our *niche* of interacting in the world, to figure out how to take the bit of currency that the master gave us and turn it into something else of value. A person with only one currency (one thing to exchange) might multiply the one thing ten times. A person with five things to exchange might multiply each of those things by two. The result is that both people received something to exchange, and both people produced ten times as much! Again, the parable is not about the quantity of currency or even *how much* of what is produced. It is about *using* the currency so that it produces something more... something of value to God.

For example, Billy Graham's adult children have some currency in the world. I can also see that they each take what God gave them individually (including skills and ways of doing things) and they exchange their *currency* (which might be their father's fame) to produce something that glorifies God. Think about it. Franklin Graham has visionary skills, organizational skills, and a heart to take the love of Christ to people with needs. Ann Graham Lotz has skills in writing and speaking, and she uses them positively in educating and inspiring others in God's kingdom. Through the currency God deposited in their lives, each of these people uses individual means and skills to produce more in God's kingdom.

We, too, have some currency from God. We can use our means and skills to turn our currency into something that uniquely creates value in God's kingdom. Each of us has something God gave us to *exchange*. We are to take whatever currency God places in our lives and use our means and skills to *invest* it in the world for more value. Each of *us* has *currency*. Social connections, experiences we have had, trials we have faced, languages we speak, visibility, blocks of time, or circumstances, for instance, are special forms of currency that we can exchange. We also have certain kinds of skills, and we have our unique ways of doing things. We may even have a Barnabas trait or two we could consistently use so what we *have* not only multiplies *our* mission but the missions of *others* as well.

That is my idea of investment. Whatever God places in us shouldn't stay in us. It needs to come out into the world to play. It needs to come out into the world to be exchanged for more profit in God's kingdom.

Barnabas Component 4: Facilitation

Facilitation is about making something easier. The word *facilitation* originates from the Latin words *facilis and facere*.

Facilis means easy, and *facere* means to make, do, or accomplish. Any time a person collaborates with people or processes to make parts work together more easily, he acts as a facilitator. A facilitator uses his skills to get something done!

Examine again this example from a previous component:

> *"You were incredible in that meeting. It was amazing how you managed communication so that everyone in that room could have their views and concerns understood by the other people. People who usually do not even listen to other people suddenly understood what was important to others and why."*

The person observed in this example *is* a facilitator. This person made it easy for the parts of a decision process to function effectively. He also helped people on the committee to consider other points of view. His communication skills allowed people to see all the parts of an issue so they could make effective decisions about it.

Consider a machine with multiple parts. A car, for instance, has many kinds of parts. If those parts work without consideration of other parts, the car might run for a while, but it will break down at some point because adverse friction will occur if all parts are not working in synchronization with each other. Likewise, if there are multiple steps, organizations, or people involved in a process, facilitation will create a process flow to make efforts easier and more likely to succeed. A Barnabas facilitator is a person who can assist someone in creating and navigating steps to make a mission launch so a purpose can be fulfilled.

A person might be a Barnabas facilitator if he can connect a person with training, provide resources, or integrate someone into an existing process. He might also be a facilitator if he can connect a person to someone who might have information about financing, logistics, coordination, or other operational issues. Barnabas facilitators are people who observe constantly, see the parts of a process, listen, communicate, and make things work together more efficiently.

Barnabas Component 5: Encouragement

I love the story called *The Elephant Rope*. A man walked by a group of enormous, powerful elephants and noticed that tiny ropes attached to only one foot tethered them in place. Perplexed, the man approached a nearby trainer to ask how this was possible. The trainer explained it was because he applied the ropes when the elephants were babies. When the elephants were little, the ropes could easily hold them in place. Curiously, as they grew to adulthood, the elephants' perceptions of themselves did not grow, so the rope still held them captive even though a simple lifting of the foot would have set them free.

Encouragement is putting courage *in* someone. It does the two things that would have set those elephants free! Encouragement can:

- change *perceptions* that hold someone back, and
- cause someone to *lift a foot*.

We have already discussed the vast array of perceptions that Satan can use to immobilize people and keep them from the purpose God has for them. Encouragers must battle toxic thinking with targeted words and actions. Can we discern what idea held by the person is interfering with his efficacy? Do we need to change his beliefs about himself or other people? Changing his outlook on how other people view him may be a pivotal step, and it may create a path to release power within him. The person may need a change of view about a problem he is facing, or another perspective about his capability.

Many people find themselves tethered to notions of having nothing to offer or they don't feel connected. They may feel inferior or think others *view* them as inferior. They may not recognize their abilities, or they don't think people in the church like them or care about them. Have we even considered that they might just need a genuine invitation?

Remember, encouragement is fuel. People everywhere need others to fill them up with the fuel of encouragement. They need a real person to help them pick up a foot and take a step toward the purpose God designed them to carry out. Encouragers should pay attention to people everywhere they go. They should notice when people are doing something well and let them know with words more powerful than *good job*. Telling a person *what* they did well and how it *affected* someone or how their actions *helped* invites people to keep using their gifts. It lets them know they make a significant difference.

Encouragers notice when people don't seem to have their usual energy, and they find out why. They talk to people and find out what they are experiencing physically, emotionally, and spiritually. To give someone words of support, encouragers might take the time to write a letter or a note. They might give someone a gentle push to take another step, or maybe they take someone for coffee so they can pour them a tall cup of motivation. Encouragers might even request someone's help just to applaud their skills. They schedule time to be in their company, engage in conversations, and find opportunities to boost their confidence.

Encouragement is important in getting people started and in keeping them going. When I was teaching guidance lessons in classrooms, kids would often start cheering or clapping when I entered their rooms. Perhaps they were only glad to avoid doing math for the next thirty minutes, but that response always encouraged me to be a better teacher. It inspired me to prepare more diligently and to present more enthusiastically. It made all the difference. When I visited groups of kids for the first time, I would often say, "When your eyes are on me and you are listening and working with me, it makes me teach better!" I was not lying. Their encouragement definitely made me teach better. The fuel we gather from others makes a difference.

To conclude, it would be helpful to read and absorb these three scriptures:

> *"Each of us should please our neighbors for their good, to build them up."*
>
> (Romans 15:2)

> *"And let us consider how we may spur one another on toward love and good deeds, not giving up meeting together, as some are in the habit of doing, but encouraging one another-and all the more as you see the Day approaching."*
>
> (Hebrews 10:24-25)

> *"Encourage one another and build one another up, just as you are doing."*
>
> (I Thessalonians 5:11)

The apostle Paul had quite a lot to say about encouragement, and I am fairly sure it was because he had a friend like Barnabas who freely gave it to *him*.

Barnabas Component 6: The Art of Invitation

This component does not appear in the Barnabas Effect definition, but for those who genuinely want to be Barnabas people, it is certainly implied. Please understand that a Barnabas invitation is not about words. It is about *escorting* people. "We would love for you to come to the fellowship supper" is not an invitation. It is just a *tease* that makes people think there is an invitation coming but then disappoints them into *not* showing up.

People are most likely to take risks in new situations when they perceive two things: 1. support and 2. accompaniment. Remember, Barnabas people don't just say "Happy Trails!" They say, "I'll walk *with* you." A real invitation tells people you are interested in them and that you want to *escort* them into a new situation and *connect* them to norms, procedures, and other people. A real invitation tells people that someone will be their concierge into *comfort* in a new situation. Here is an example:

> *"I'd like to get you and your wife connected in our Wednesday Night GROW Program! Can you come this Wednesday? I would like to meet you at the south door and escort you through the supper line. I want you to sit at the table with me and my wife so we can introduce you to people.*
>
> *You can try our GROW group this week, and I'll introduce you to the leaders of other GROW groups so that you can visit other ones later, if you choose. I'll make sure you have some information about all the different available studies, too. Do you think you could come this week at 5:30 on Wednesday? Great! I will wait for you at the south door."*

An invitation should tell people they *are wanted*. There should be a commitment to *walk with* them through the new situation and show them how to operate in it. A promise should be included to answer questions, give needed information, and provide introductions to other people. A Barnabas-style invitation could even offer to accompany someone for an extended period until they feel comfortable and connected.

And what about invitations to get people involved in a mission or a work project? You may know the group of people you are talking to, or at least some of them, but the same rules of invitation apply! An announcement that "work is going to begin next week at a shelter home, and if you wish to help, just let Bob know" is *not* an invitation! Here is how that should go.

Our church will begin work at a new shelter home this week. Specifically, this week we are going to be doing some basic framing to stand a structure up. We need people who can:

- *use nail guns*
- *measure and mark accurately*
- *use a power saw*
- *help lift wall sections*
- *do site cleanup*
- *take pictures or videos of the work*
- *bring lunch and drinks to the site for the workers*

If you think you could do any of these things on Thursday, Friday, or from 8:00 to 1:00 this Saturday, please raise your hand right now and let the ushers hand you a flyer with some specific information. If you are still interested after you look at the information, please meet me in the fellowship hall right after church, and I will answer questions you have and get you signed up for whatever tasks you can do on whichever days you can work. My personal phone number is also on that flyer, so if you cannot stay right after church, you can call me or text me. We will do various kinds of work as we go, so if this week will not work for you or if the things we have going on do not match your skill set, you can still get involved later. I will make weekly announcements and meet with folks each Sunday after church who want to help the following week. Please raise your hand if you think you even might be interested, and we will get you information on how you can help with construction tasks, cleanup, media documentation, or feeding our workers.

This invitation strategy gives people the information they need to *engage*. Notice that there is a way to learn details and to decide *if* they can engage. There is a time and a place to converse specifically about the mission opportunity and to learn more. Finally, information gets in the hands of potential workers, and it includes specific contact information for the person in charge of organizing the project.

Make no mistake. There is an art and a science to creating invitations that produce results. Carefully crafting invitations can be a critical factor in the success of all kinds of Barnabas ventures.

Chapter 19

Designing a Barnabas Church That Connects People to Purpose

To begin this topic, I simply suggest that people are always key. A Barnabas church begins with Barnabas people, who are consistently using Barnabas behaviors to do Barnabas work. I hope the ideas in this book will help people employ those incredibly important strategies. I also hope that Barnabas people will think about those Barnabas questions we have talked about before and intentionally wonder about every person they meet in the church. I hope they ask themselves,

What does this person have in him that God wants to use?

and

How can I connect him to his God-given mission and purpose?

I believe that when Christians seek answers to these questions, they will want to strategize about how their church can create an environment where people are carried to purpose. This chapter attempts to stimulate *your* thinking about *your* church so that your ideas will lead to kingdom fruit. I want to do this through three topics that include 1) discovery, 2) apprenticeship, and 3) structure as preparation for confidence.

Discovery

A fundamental role of a Barnabas church will be to help people understand their unique attributes and connect those to ministry areas. However, this process is not as simple as creating inspirational moments, taking an inventory, or completing a checklist about where a person wants to serve. Personal discovery is a complex, emerging process. It is a lifelong journey, full of twists and turns that challenge our understanding of ourselves and our world. It is both organic and dynamic. Growing, breathing, and changing shape over time, it continues to respond to the experiences and emotions that make us who we are. More importantly, it is spiritual. At its core, personal discovery is a quest for meaning and connection. It is a plunge into the soul to discover God's purpose expressed in our lives and the passions it produces.

I would love to design a course that could connect people with their God-given purposes. While it is possible to plan and structure some specific experiences that would open individuals to a better understanding of themselves and their relationship to their God-given mission, I contend that any course would only begin the process. You see, my experience tells me that while people have individual tendencies, their natural predispositions are not completely *static*. They flex and change! They can be amazingly fluid, and they can shift drastically when the surrounding environment is conducive.

In my work with students, I have seen severely timid students become accomplished speakers. I have seen incredibly shy students take the stage and play a brilliant role. I have also seen extremely individualistic kids suddenly become amazing leaders who could integrate with others and pull a group into a successful enterprise. When the Bible refers to us as clay, it certainly describes the innate pliability in each of us.

What I know unequivocally about people is that they have capacity far beyond what they display and far beyond what they have discovered in themselves. You can send a person down a path, but what they meet on the journey will often determine how they will evolve and what they will become. Gideon, after all, was just stomping around in a pit but changed directions when an angel called him a *mighty warrior*. What he was doing made no sense. He was trying to thresh wheat in a winepress! His circumstances held his productivity and his potential hostage.

As a church that wants to activate what is inert and put it to work in God's kingdom, we must remember two important biblical constructs. First, God can use who and what He chooses, and He often chooses the most unlikely. Second, he can create anything that is needed with His mighty hand. Therefore, we definitely should design learning experiences that move people to think about who they are and to pray about what roles they can pursue in Christ's mission. However, we shouldn't get too cocky about any method other than the one God chooses. Our goal should be to invite people into a mindset of service, to convey that we are certain of their unique potential as God's instruments, and to help them get into a relationship with God that will precipitate their mobilization.

It is prudent at this point to mention that there is unfortunate confusion about how God-given gifts and God-given purposes translate into service. Often, if a person wants to do something in the church, the good people in the church will immediately turn the focus toward open *holes* that need to be filled. Then they will try to stuff that person into an available hole. If a person says he wants to get involved, someone is likely to say,

> "Great! We need a teacher for the third graders."

> OR

> "The Smiths just moved. We now need another usher."

There is no thought about who the person is, what his talents are, or where he is on his spiritual journey. We need to fill those holes!

Do not misunderstand me. I recognize some tasks are necessary for the daily operations of the church. However, tasks and personal ministry are not the same thing. Maybe, just maybe, we could do better at moving people into more authentic, personal discipleship. Here is what I believe:

> *People don't just need to fill a spot.*
>
> *They need to find a purpose.*

I repeat:

People don't just need to fill a spot.

They need to find a purpose!

All of that said, the challenge to churches is to move beyond the tendency toward just *assigning* tasks. Instead, the church should move toward *designing* experiences where people can discover where God wants to use them. When people come to salvation, they should also come to the knowledge that they are each fearfully and wonderfully made to glorify God by fulfilling their God-given purposes. That knowledge will then spark these two pivotal questions:

What *is* my God-given purpose?

and

How will I know when I am fulfilling it?

In his book *Why You Can't Be Anything You Want to Be*, Arthur Miller grapples with both these questions. He speaks of striving as a new Christian to discover what a person does with his life after he is born again into a relationship with God. At the time of his struggle, Miller, although trained as a lawyer, just could not wrap his natural tendencies around typical work in the legal profession. Instead, he found ways to incorporate those tendencies in his job, and, through a series of events, he eventually landed in personnel development, not law. In that field, he flourished. He also developed a unique system for helping people find their specific vocational strengths based on what he calls *natural motivated ability patterns*. In his work, he also answered his personal question about what it means to glorify God with the life you live.

What does it mean to glorify God in your life?

Miller answers the question this way:

> "It is using one's endowed giftedness to serve the world with excellence and, through that service, to love and honor God."

The discovery process in churches should seek to help each Christian do just what Miller described. It should help people explore the gifts expressed in their natural tendencies and connect those gifts to what they do in daily life, inside and outside the church. And how does one know when he is right in the middle of his God-given purpose? Well, my experience tells me that a person can sometimes get fortuitously lost in his work. He then notices a sense of pleasure followed by occasional moments of all-out euphoria. More simply, he finds *JOY* in what he is doing. Wouldn't it be extraordinary to lead people in our churches to *that*?

Apprenticeship

During the years I spent in elementary classrooms, I noticed small but intriguing changes in the general information students gleaned from the world around them. One of those changes I want to point out here is a tiny shift with a significant connection to this book.

As a school counselor, I often had conversations with children in classrooms about what their parents did for *work*. In my early career, children answered pretty accurately with the title of their parents' occupations. They could also describe at least something about what kinds of tasks their moms and dads did during their workday. Today, however, many children do not know what their parents do to make a living. If they can even identify the name of a company where the parent works, they rarely know what the parent does on the job. I mention this observation to highlight a notable change in the way our society moves children into adult life.

Not so long ago, children were a part of family enterprise from the time they could walk and talk. Often, they helped in a family business or worked in an agricultural venture. They did chores, or they assisted in those being done by parents and siblings. Young people walked beside their parents and worked beside them as they carried out daily work. They saw their parents struggle, encounter difficulties, and solve problems. Children watched parents help others, and they also watched them as they communicated, cooperated, and negotiated with others. Through observation and participation, children learned how to do essential tasks and how to interact with a variety of other people connected to their daily lives. From birth, they were in apprenticeship to become capable adults.

In the Bible, the concept of apprenticeship is also central and fundamental to the development of God's human instruments. Joshua was in a calculated apprenticeship with Moses. He saw every step and every stumble of his mentor. Elisha was immersed in an ordained, step-by-step internship with Elijah, and twelve unlikely men experienced a mentorship like none other with Jesus. It is interesting, too, that all these apprentices we have mentioned received a command to increase the mission. Joshua was to take his people farther than they had ever been as an organized nation. Elisha produced exactly twice as many miracles as Elijah. And what did Jesus say to his disciples?

> *"Very truly I tell you, whoever believes in me will do the works I have been doing, and they will do even greater things than these, because I am going to the Father. And I will do whatever you ask in my name, so that the Father may be glorified in the Son."*
>
> (John 14:12-13)

Mentorship produces something valuable. When people increase their *competence*, they also increase their *confidence* and their abilities to take on new ventures, new roles, and new enterprises. Apprenticeship is not necessarily about getting a person on board with a mission someone else has designed. It can be a preparatory step for spawning new missions. The apprentice relationship forms a crucible to create new capabilities, new missions, and new purposes. Showing others how a mission operates in tangible, everyday terms is transitional to generating new enterprises and outcomes. The process is like playing *dress-up*. It allows people to be in a safe environment to try on roles, practice methods, and experience ways of negotiating the world so they can see what best fits their tendencies.

Apprenticeship places people in a position to explore the passions of others and to experience the ways people deliver their purposes to the world around them. Walking in the footsteps of another can inspire fresh paths and different purposes. It can also provide skills that transfer to other journeys.

So, I throw this simple question out to churches that want to activate people in pursuit of God-given missions and purposes. Could apprenticeship play a role? Could churches create internships to give people short-term experiences that might spawn ideas and point to ways for people to use their gifts? Would people who engage in specific missions be willing to take on a protégé and walk with the person, pray for him, and encourage his search for direction?

Structure As Preparation for Confidence

Think back, for a moment, to the Gallup survey mentioned in Chapter 7. In that survey, there was a large component of people who stated that they were not involved in Christian ministry because they either did not know how or no one had asked them. Others had no interest in being involved in ministry. If the Christian church is to reclaim its resources for God's purposes, it must carefully target and address all three issues. Churches can teach people how to engage. Churches can learn how to invite people into service, and with the right strategies, they can even develop interest. Christ's church has the responsibility to create engagement by inviting people into knowledge about the spiritual mission (*bechora*) and resources (*berachot*) that come with salvation. Churches also need to build confidence that comes from a spiritual foundation and a spiritual motivation to pursue a mission.

As we move forward with *Barnabas* intention, there are two pressing matters we should consider. First, it would be great to get more people who are *outside* the church to move *inside* the church. Churches today have more of a tendency to *shuffle and deal* the same church people around to different church buildings than to bring in people from outside the church who need to know Jesus. Second, the way we assimilate people into churches should not look like how we get a membership card for Sam's Club. It should cause people to become a part of the fabric and intention of God's family and God's mission.

In many churches, the flow of spiritual development functions rather like a car wash. In the first phase, people get washed, and after that, there are options to get waxed, get shined, and keep the trash out. Often, the idea is some attendants serve as gurus in each phase, and the rest of the people just stay on the conveyor belt so they can come out cleaner and shinier.

It is also quite common for people in churches to see themselves as unprepared for service. Many would say that they do not have adequate knowledge about the Bible or the foundational beliefs of their faith. Because of those deficits, they would also say they feel unprepared to witness to others or work in church endeavors. Could it be that people lack preparation and that causes a subsequent lack of confidence? Perhaps it is a lack of preparation and confidence that causes them to assign themselves to the spectator seats. Could it be that people do not see themselves as capable of adding value, so they choose inactivity or anonymity?

Confidence makes a human being more effective. It is not arrogance or superiority. It is an inner perception of value and capability that helps a person interact with the world more boldly and more successfully. Real confidence, however, emerges through equipping. It requires a person to learn basic functional information, acquire skills for seeking and applying information, and develop proficiency for managing experiences.

Because the most confident people I know are military personnel and veterans of the military, I explored what these people have in common. My research produced two incredibly significant conclusions. In a nutshell, *military recruits study the military, and the military studies them.* All recruits gain a common core of knowledge and skills, and then the military conducts a discovery process to determine the unique characteristics of each recruit and how those can be valuable to the military.

Recently, I ran across an article celebrating the 385th anniversary of the National Guard and I read about how the organization operates. The members of the National Guard are citizens from all *walks of life* who work in the civilian world until called upon to serve in a domestic situation or a military mission. Service might occur in a neighborhood close to home or anywhere around the world. To describe this organization further, it has both a unique mission and a unique organization. Distinctively, these everyday citizens are *highly and exceptionally trained* to provide critical service upon demand.

It occurs to me that the mission of the National Guard has many similarities with the mission of the church. The church, too, has a commission to provide for the needs of people close to home. It is further ordained to take the gospel to all nations as it delivers Godly love to those same people. However, the question to ponder is whether most churches could say their membership is highly and exceptionally trained to provide the service it is called to deliver.

If we examine the training design of the National Guard, we can identify four phases. The first two phases provide a core of common information and essential skills. The topics in these two phases are:

- core values
- weapons training
- combat training
- fitness training
- map and compass skills
- inspection readiness
- self-discipline training
- team maneuvering

After basic training, recruits learn to execute a specific army job based on individual strengths. Finally, recruits receive advanced training that prepares them to become occupational field experts in supervisory, leadership, or management roles. When all the initial training is complete, the organization commits to ongoing training for all personnel that occurs at regular intervals. To summarize, the National Guard requires

- a *common core* of experiences
- training about what is *fundamental* for all
- *individualized training* based on individual strengths
- *advanced training* to connect developed talents and skills to domestic and broader issues

Throughout the training sequence, there is a specific ratio of recruits to training officers, so preparation is *highly accompanied*, and recruits are essentially *escorted* into effective service.

Like the National Guard, the church has a highly critical and important mission. Shouldn't the personnel be just as deliberately and intentionally trained for confident service? Perhaps the church could create strategic phases for every member to

- acquire a basic, *common core* of knowledge about the Bible
- gain a working knowledge of foundational theological beliefs and the local church's vision
- develop the essential skills of spiritual warfare, spiritual self-inspection, self-discipline, and Christian team maneuvering
- discover the relationship between individual gifts, purpose, and mission
- determine how personal gifts translate to Christian service
- access specialized training to develop one's gifts for purposes inside and outside the church

The suggestion here is that all members should have a common base of training that is delivered upon membership. Confidence comes from learning and preparation, and productivity comes from confidence. Deliberate strategic equipping is key. How many more people could become potent in Christ's mission with access to targeted training?

I am certainly not the first person to suggest a more structured approach to church membership training. Some churches have developed impactful phases for discipleship training, and there are many excellent models to compare. I am suggesting, though, that churches could consider how providing a common experience of assimilation might create a more *Barnabas-like* atmosphere. Could we produce more fruit if we could tweak the usual paradigm for bringing people into the church and *walking with them* throughout their lives? What would happen if churches guided people not only to salvation but also to their specific *purposes* for kingdom work?

Remember:

Bechora: leadership, mission.

Mission: God's plan to bring the people He loves to Himself.

Berachot: all the resources needed to accomplish the mission.

In designing a Barnabas church, *nurturing, assimilating, equipping,* and *developing* God's people for kingdom work should remain central. Mining the potential of every member should become a crucial part of that process as well. When the church leaves these tasks to happenstance, it loses much in treasure, talent, and *efficacy*. Sometimes, there is even a reduction to only 10 percent of its people who are engaging in personal ministry! *(Remember Chapter 7?)*

Hear this:

> *Inviting people into commitment is not a deterrent.*
>
> *It is a magnet!*

In this chapter, I have made suggestions about bringing people into the family and the mission of the church through a common system of deliberate and structured assimilation. I have done that in words. Words create ideas, and ideas inspire construction. Construction then produces something to deliver. I am simply asking readers to let my words inspire your journey toward *powering up for purpose*.

Your church will not become a *Barnabas Church* overnight! However, all churches can start somewhere and do something. People can learn more about themselves, their God-given talents, and ways to use their gifts in kingdom work. Churches can teach that God can use anyone and everyone whose heart is tuned to Him.

Chapter 20

Conclusion: Seeds Need Help

While working on this book, I discovered a modern English translation of the Bible called the Passion Translation, written to unlock God's passion and His intense love for mankind. When I explored its language, I could not help but fall in love with the way it expresses Ephesians 4:16. The beautiful words that flow there are these:

> *"For His "body" has been formed in His image and is closely joined together and constantly connected as one. And every member has been given divine gifts to contribute to the growth of all; and as these gifts operate effectively throughout the whole body, we are built up and made perfect in love."*

If you have read this book, I believe purpose is on your heart. I would also suppose that you believe God has planted seeds of purpose in every one of His children. Unfortunately, the Bible tells us that seeds face opposition of all kinds. The enemy comes and plants weeds, as it says in Matthew 13:25, and because the conditions around seeds can dry them out, choke them out, let them die from malnutrition, or leave them vulnerable to pests that destroy them, *seeds need help.*

Around the time I read the beautiful scripture above, I came across some fascinating information about sustainable farming. I learned that one of the current best practices in that field is an agricultural technique called *intercropping*. This practice, in simple terms, requires planting two or more crops together for mutual benefit. The technique itself makes crops much less attractive to pests and weeds, and some plants even have specific attributes to defend plants from intruders. More interesting, however, are the interdependent relationships that are beneficial. Stalk plants, for instance, can provide a structure for vine plants to grow on. Other plants can provide wind protection for companion plants. Some plants offer natural ground cover, which secures moisture for neighboring flora, and other plants provide shade. Certain planting patterns increase soil nutrients or manage their use, and other groupings impact the efficient use of water and light. Planting and growing multiple species together can achieve both efficient use of land and synergy in ecological processes. The result is a higher yield.

God wants His people to produce fruit of all kinds. They all need to grow in a place where they receive nourishment and have access to the Light of the World and Living Water. They might also need specific help from others, such as structure, protection from the winds that blow in daily life, and loving defense against pests that destroy. I am convinced that Christian people, like plants, can benefit from an environment where diverse gifts grow in tandem. Every gift that is developed supports and fortifies others. The challenge, however, is to create an ecosystem that will not only allow people to grow together but also produce higher yields in kingdom work.

Christ's church can be a better steward of the *seeds of purpose* planted in people for kingdom work. To embrace that calling, it must create a community that encourages human beings to function better in their unique designs. It must provide an environment where gifts, talents, and energies can flourish, so people can pursue kingdom tasks more effectively.

The apostle Barnabas provides a picture of a priest ordained with an extraordinary mission. He dedicated himself to the cultivation of treasures God placed in people for His purposes. As we apply processes that create the Barnabas Effect, we, too, can become holy stewards of the potential in God's uniquely designed people. We can grow the gifts He placed in people and produce beautiful Kingdom fruit.

Reader, thank you for taking this journey with me. I hope you find Barnabas power in yourself and that you experience it from those around you. And finally, my prayer for you is this: As you find your beautiful God-given purpose and use it for His glory, may it bring you pure *JOY*.

> *"But you are a chosen people, a royal priesthood, a holy nation, God's special possession, that you may declare the praises of him who called you out of darkness into his wonderful light."*
>
> (1 Peter 2:9)

Bibliography

Boice, James. "Moses' Early Education." Alliance of Confessing Evangelicals, http://alliance@alliancenet.org. June 2024.

Branch, Robin. "Barnabas: Early Church Leader and Model of Encouragement," *In the Scripture Light/In Luce Verbi*, Vol 41, no 2, AOSIS, July 2007.

Branch, Robin. "Barnabas: An Encouraging Early Church Leader." *Bible History Daily,* 2007, www.biblicalarcheology.org.

Chatterlee, Rhitu. "Americans Are Lonely A lot, and Young People Bear the Heaviest Burden." NPR, 1 May 2018, http://npr.org

Congleton, Christina. "Mindfulness Can Literally Change Your Brain." Harvard Business Review. Harvard Business School Publishing Corporation, Jan. 2015.

Cuncic, Arlin. "How To Develop and Practice Self Regulation." VeryWellMind, May 2023.

Eysenck, Michael W. *Simply Psychology*. Psychology Press, 2012.

Frankl, Viktor E. *Man's Search for Meaning*. Beacon Press, 2006.

"Loneliness In America: Making Caring Common." Harvard School of Education, 2020.

Majid, Fotuhi and Mehr, Sara. "The Science Behind the Practical Benefits of Having a Purpose." Practical Neurology, Sept. 2015. https://practical neurology.com.

Miller, Arthur F. *Why You Can't Be Anything You Want to Be*. Zondervan Publishing House, 1999.

Riskin, Schlomo. "Parshat Toldot: Brothers, Birthrights, and Blessings." *Jerusalem Post*, Nov. 2006.

"Our Epidemic of Loneliness and Isolation: The U.S. Surgeon General's Advisory on the Healing Effects of Social Connection and Community, 2023." *U.S. Department of Health and Human Services, 12. Office of the U.S. Surgeon General, 2023*.

"Know More, Live Brighter." *VeryWellMind, 2018*. http://verywellmind.com

Warren, Rick. *The Purpose Driven Church*. Zondervan, 2007.

Easton's Bible Dictionary. London: T. Nelson and Sons, 1897.

Bible Translations Referenced

King James Version (KJV)

The New King James Version (NKJV)

New International Version (NIV)

The Message (MSG)

The Passion Translation (TPT)

New International Reader's Version (NIrV)

Good News Translation (GNT)

New American Standard Bible (NASB)

New Living Translation (NLV)

The Voice (Voice)

English Standard Version (ESV)

More Resources

More on Metacognitive Questions

Metacognitive questions are questions that increase people's understanding of what is going on in their heads and their hearts! These questions help individuals and groups to notice their own thought processes so they can see where their thoughts are leading them or possibly how their thoughts are preventing their progress. Metacognitive exploration of thought can:

- aid focus and planning
- help people who are stuck to move
- help people monitor their goals and stay on track
- help people achieve better results for both the present and the future by examining experiences and thoughts that get in the way

Encouraging people to think about their thinking can help them solve problems, become more creative in their approaches to tasks, and improve results. People can reflect on choices, understand causes and effects, and notice factors that lead to successful outcomes. Learning to use these powerful questions can move others to be more and accomplish more. Metacognitive questions do not direct or boss people. They encourage and empower! They seek to free people for joyful obedience to their purposes.

Most importantly, asking metacognitive questions is a great way to show genuine interest in other people so they feel seen and valued. Metacognitive questions also give insight to the person who is asking the questions. Why? Because the more each of us understands the other, the more we can use what we have inside us to bring forth purpose in both ourselves and others!

Examples of Metacognitive Questions

- What are you observing/noticing in that situation?
- What is new about…?
- What about this situation makes you think about another situation?
- How can you connect that to…?
- What questions are coming to your mind in this situation?
- Why is that issue important to you?
- What do you know for sure?
- What is something you need to know or would like to know about this situation before you act?
- What obstacles are you experiencing?
- What steps have you taken so far?
- What did you learn about yourself when you were going through that experience?
- What do you think keeps you from…?
- What thoughts go through your head when someone asks you to…?
- When you see others _____, what goes through your mind?
- You said you hesitated. What made you go ahead and…?

- What would you want someone to say or to do that would help you take that step?
- What got in your way so that you did not _____?
- Could you see yourself...?
- Have you thought about....?
- When did you do something you did not think you could?
- When has an obstacle or setback actually worked to help you?
- Can you describe a time when you felt listened to or a time someone really heard you?
- What is something you would like to take with you from that experience?
- What is something you could leave behind that would help you travel better on this journey?
- What are some things people have done to gain your trust?
- What ideas did you have?
- What is your trust level right now?
- What are some things you admire in others?
- What gets in your way when you consider something you want to do or need to do?
- What are some things people do that make you feel comfortable in trusting them?
- What questions do you ask yourself when you are comparing yourself to others?
- What is something you feel really good about right now?
- What would you do differently if you had that experience again?
- Tell me about a decision you made this week. What factors did you consider in making that decision?
- What were you thinking when _____?
- How do you think people see you? What words describe how you think other people see you?

- What role do you usually take in _____?
- What roles would you like to try?
- What decision did you finally make and how did that work out?
- Give me three words that say what holds you back.
- What's working for you right now? What is definitely not working for you right now?
- Can you describe/show me what that looks like when it occurs?
- Can you give me an example of when that has happened?
- Tell me about an example of when that happened.
- What are you thinking right now since I brought up this possibility?
- What do you really want to do that no one has asked you to do?
- Can you see anything changing?
- What steps did you take ?
- What do you think caused the problem?
- What do you want to happen?
- What do you want someone to do that would really help?
- Where did you get stuck in that?
- What happened last time?
- What past experience keeps you from taking risks?

www.ingramcontent.com/pod-product-compliance
Lightning Source LLC
Chambersburg PA
CBHW061208070526
44583CB00025B/3161